BARTERING
WITH THE BONES
OF THEIR DEAD

FRANKLIN D. ROOSEVELT LAKE AND SOUTH END OF THE COLVILLE RESERVATION FROM THE WILBUR GRADE ON HIGHWAY 21

Bartering with the Bones of Their Dead

THE COLVILLE CONFEDERATED TRIBES AND TERMINATION

LAURIE ARNOLD

UNIVERSITY OF WASHINGTON PRESS

Seattle & London

This publication is made possible in part by
support from the University of Notre Dame.

© 2012 by the University of Washington Press
Printed and bound in the United States of America
Design by Thomas Eykemans
Composed in Chaparral, typeface designed by Carol Twombly
16 15 14 13 12   5 4 3 2 1

All photographs are by Laurie Arnold.

UNIVERSITY OF WASHINGTON PRESS
PO Box 50096, Seattle, WA 98145, USA
www.washington.edu/uwpress

LIBRARY OF CONGRESS CATALOGING-IN-PUBLICATION DATA
Arnold, Laurie.
Bartering with the bones of their dead : the Colville Confederated tribes and termination /
Laurie Arnold.
    p. cm.
Includes bibliographical references and index.
ISBN 978-0-295-99198-6 (cloth : alk. paper)
ISBN 978-0-295-99228-0 (pbk. : alk. paper)
1. Confederated Tribes of the Colville Reservation, Washington—History. 2. Colville Indi-
ans—Legal status, laws, etc.—Washington (State)—Colville Indian Reservation. 3. Colville
Indians—Government relations. 4. Colville Indians—Politics and government. 5. Indian
termination policy—Washington (State)—Colville Indian Reservation. 6. Self-determination, National—Washington (State)—Colville Indian Reservation. 7. Colville Indian Reservation (Wash.)—History. 8. Colville Indian Reservation (Wash.) I. Title.
E99.C844.A75 2012   979.7'28—dc23   2012012666

They have always refused to enter into any agreement in regard to the disposition or sale of their lands; refused to be bound by the Government or other tribes who they regard as interlopers on their lands and they have consistently held to this. They announced then as they have always done that if the entire million and a half dollars were piled on the floor in front of them and they were told to help themselves not a penny of it would they accept. They stoutly claim ownership of the lands on which they have lived for generations and would not sell for any price but acknowledge the right of other tribes to barter with the graves and bones of their dead.

JOHN MCADAMS WEBSTER
writing about the San Poil band of
Colville Indians, 1906

For my parents

CONTENTS

State of Washington featuring the Colville Indian Reservation

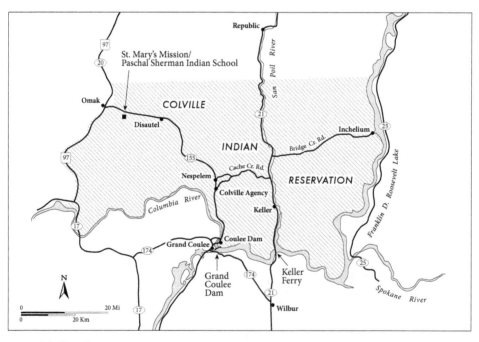

Colville Indian Reservation

PREFACE

Upon passage of termination legislation in 1953, Congress believed that the United States had entered a new phase in management of Indian affairs. Previous policies, including removal, allotment, and the Indian Reorganization Act (IRA), in many ways reinforced federal responsibility to and management of recognized Indian tribes, but termination was considered the tool that would finally end US involvement with and commitments to Indians.

When both houses of Congress passed House Concurrent Resolution 108 in August of 1953, its proponents believed that they had ushered in a new day for Indians and for the US government. The language of what became known as the termination bill called for "Indians within the territorial limits of the United States to be subject to the same laws and entitled to the same privileges and responsibilities as are applicable to other citizens of the United States." More importantly, the bill called for the end of Indians' unique wardship status, and asserted that they "should assume their full responsibilities as American Citizens."[1] The men who drafted the legislation believed the process would be a simple and relatively speedy one: experts would go to reservations to assess the value of land, mineral, and human resources, and Congress would tally those figures to create a lump sum value that would be paid to tribal members of that group on a per capita basis. The process could then be repeated for each of the hundreds of tribal groups in the United States in 1953. While Indians would still live in America, the government would no longer recognize tribal groups and would have no further responsibility to them as groups or as individuals.

In fact, many of the termination processes turned out to be exceedingly complex and very costly. The Menominee Tribe of Wisconsin and the Klamath Tribe of Oregon remain the two best-known examples of terminated tribes. Both were identified in the original bill and were to have completed their termination process within five years. Instead, both encountered considerable difficulties as they tried to implement this new policy, and both tribes were officially terminated in 1961, eight years after passage of H.C.R. 108. The Menominees had a strong government and were highly self-sufficient. They owned and operated their own utilities, a saw mill, and a clothing factory. Income from these operations, as well as from their timber resources, paid the Bureau of Indian Affairs (BIA) costs associated with the Menominee Reservation. The tribe also had surplus funds on deposit. In other words, the Menominees were a sound economic and political organization. Even so, tribal leaders did not favor complete termination of ties with the federal government, and had grave concerns that the tribe and its members were not prepared to operate without some oversight from the BIA.

These concerns proved to be valid. After a long lead-up to termination, legislation officially severing ties between the Menominee Tribe and the US government was passed in 1961, and the Menominees were on their own. In a relatively short span of years, their operations spun out of control. They lost many of their holdings and most of their real estate (including property owned by individuals) because, as a corporation, they owed taxes. Never having paid taxes, few individuals had cash to do so, and many had to liquidate holdings or lose their property to tax sales. People who had never been on relief had to join the welfare rolls. Only a decade after being targeted for termination, members of this once-stable group found themselves without income, resources, or land.

The Klamaths faced a worse fate, because they had fewer operational resources, high unemployment, and a less-organized tribal government. The Klamath termination process dragged on primarily because federal officials could not agree with timber companies on a fair price for the Klamaths' massive timber resources, and because a small group of Klamaths wanted to remain on their lands instead of taking the per capita payment. Finally, in 1961, Congress passed legislation terminating the Klamath Tribe, approving what would result in a $43,000 payment to each tribal member.

Although both the Menominee and the Klamath tribes eventually regained their tribal status through restoration (the Menominee in 1973 and the Klamath in 1986), neither tribe has fully recovered their land or financial resources, and members of both communities suffered intense emotional blows.

More than 100 tribes were terminated between 1953 and 1961, and, for such an important policy, termination remains a less-explored area of history and ethnohistory. Those scholars who have explored termination have enriched the field and illustrated how similar and how diverse termination experiences could be. Donald L. Fixico's *Termination and Relocation* remains the standard overview of the policy and the era. Kenneth R. Philp, in *Termination Revisited*, examines federal Indian policy from the New Deal through termination and includes some Indian responses as well.[2]

Scholarship built from the community level has added a great deal of perspective and tribal voice to termination studies on such tribes as the Confederated Salish and Kootenai Tribes of the Flathead Reservation in Montana, who successfully fought against termination; the mixed-blood Utes on the Uintah-Ouray Reservation in Utah; and the Coos, Lower Umpqua, and Siuslaw Indians of Oregon. *Menominee DRUMS* is still the best and most important monograph on restoration after termination.[3]

The Colville Tribes' story adds a new dimension to these studies.[4] It shares many similarities with other stories—legislative and BIA manipulation, tribal politicking, internal divisions, and external pressures—but the most important difference lies in the Colvilles' pursuit of termination. For nearly twenty years, between 1953 and 1972, tribal members and leaders sought to end what they considered a fictive relationship with the federal government and to return to life as citizens of their own communities, not communities the government had constructed for them. Some tribal members who favored termination asserted that their Indian identity was antimodern, and that it held them back from progressing in the white world. Others had never lived on the reservation and only sought the cash payout that termination would bring.

The stalwart opponents to termination wanted to protect the tribal identity as well as their individual identities, and they wanted to hold on to their land. They acknowledged tribal divisions among the bands, but also wanted to retain their community—constructed by outsiders or not. They envisioned a time when Colville tribal members would make greater contributions to the reservation, to the state, and to the nation, and they realized that those contributions would be informed by the Colville perspective.

In a way, the termination battle is emblematic of Colville tribal politics, and I say that as a member of the Colville Tribe. A unanimous decision by the tribal council that also represents the will of tribal members is a rarely recorded event. Disagreements do not diminish the importance of an event or a discussion, however, and often they enhance it. The disagreements over termination led to a period of growth and sophisticated political machinations unprecedented on the Colville Reservation. This painful period in tribal politics laid the foundation for the tribal institution that exists today.

My parents and I moved to Keller, Washington, in the summer of 1977. We lived for months in a single-wide trailer while contractors built our house. My parents had purchased my grandparents' home and land, and Grampa and Gramma moved to a new HUD house in town. I swam in the San Poil River nearly every day, and we hauled that same river water home to use for bathing and cooking in our temporary quarters.

Keller was a backdrop of my father's youth, and after years of being away in the army and the city (where he met my mother), he decided we should move back to the reservation. By that time, we lived in Republic, a small town just north of the reservation boundary, a place that had enjoyed a heyday as a mining town in the late 1800s and lived on in the twentieth century to serve logging interests. With a population of 1,000, Republic was positively metropolitan in comparison to Keller, whose numbers never seem to grow much beyond 300.

In Republic, my siblings had been superstars in their high school, the way kids can be in small towns. They were multisport athletes, and my sister wore the Miss Republic crown. Their popularity also enveloped me as the kid sister, and we knew almost everyone in town. Keller was a different story. I didn't know anyone, and none of my classmates cared what my brothers could do with a baseball. I also encountered a great deal of suspicion because I had moved from "the city" and was likely stuck-up as a consequence. My aunts forced my cousins to be nice to me, only worsening my situation, and I fell victim to many hair pulls and pinches. I wore a new dress to my first day of second grade in Keller. It had a white bodice with a butterfly embroidered on it and a light blue skirt; from my seven-year-old perspective, it epitomized elegance. At recess that morning, one of my cousins pushed me down and sat on me and said "No one likes city kids." Her older brother yanked her off me by one arm, smacked her, and said, "She's family! We don't hit family!" The irony of his assertion was lost on me, as I sat shocked, dusty, and tear-stained, and lamented my beautiful butterfly.

Second grade started out rough, but life got better. Our two-room schoolhouse consigned us to each other's constant company, and slowly I made friends. As we settled into our Keller lives, I learned where my dad and I came from, the Arrow Lakes band of the Colville Tribes, and how our canoe-people ancestors traversed the Columbia River, fishing and trading and traveling to see friends.

In the little round Head Start building near the post office, a friend and I spent time after school with her grandma, learning Nselxin, a Salish dialect: eagle, *milkhanoops*; owl, *sneenah*. Some of the aunties taught us girls traditional dances, and we practiced in moccasins and dance shawls in the community center gym. My daily life revolved around four buildings within a quarter mile of each other: school, post office/store, Head Start building, and community center.

My mother started beading, as a way into the often insular community. Then she taught me. We attended rodeos and celebrations across the reservation, and I loved to watch the skilled dancers bring their regalia alive as they moved. I also lived through appointments with Indian Health Service doctors and dentists and ate my fair share of government cheese, imposed upon us by the munificent BIA. Everyone called their trips to get commodities, like those five-pound blocks of cheese, "Going to Kmart."

When we returned from trips to Spokane, after sometimes visiting the real Kmart, and drove off the ferry that crosses Lake Roosevelt between the reservation and nonreservation lands, I always smiled (still do) at the sign that greeted us at the top of the hill: "Now entering the Colville Indian Reservation, 1.4 million acres."

As a child of the reservation, I learned who the Colville Tribes were, not in a formal way but through everyday conversations about grandparents and great-grandparents, mine and others, where they lived and what they used to do. There must have been classroom lessons about our history, but the knowledge I gained seems more organic to me now. I don't remember where or when I learned it, but I can tell you the history of the Colville Confederated Tribes.

As a scholar, I recognize the importance of written sources, sources documented and vetted by other scholars. As a tribal member, I am asking you to acknowledge the value of knowledge acquisition via community living. In sharing the general history of the Colvilles throughout this book, I use very few footnotes. While I have some tribal publications and education curriculum materials in my files, they list no author or publication date and they are not likely to be found outside the reservation. The Colville Tribes have a website with a section devoted to tribal history, so fact checking can be done there, but it's a timeline, not a narrative, and it offers no formal documentation.[5]

Throughout graduate school, several experienced scholars told me that I was crazy to write about my own community, understanding before I did the complexities of telling a story about my community through a scholarly lens. Perhaps they were right, but I can't imagine letting anyone else tell this great and complex tale of tribal and federal politics—it is a uniquely Colville story.

Certainly, this has not been an easy history for me to write. Readers may take a harsh view of Colville tribal members who pursued termination. They may be angered by the Colville Tribe's decision to withdraw from pan-Indian organizations when those organizations criticized the tribe's goal. Some may think the Colvilles were shortsighted, but I hope not.

The Colvilles are a confederation of twelve bands, a group of independent communities thrown together by a federal government in search of an expedient solution. One hundred and forty years ago, each of the communities had its own priorities. Is it realistic to expect that independence to have dissolved just because of a federal mandate? Most of the bands have intermarried to a great degree by now, but we still value our band identities as much as our collective identity.

Tribal members who live on the reservation may question what right I have to tell a tribal story when I have not lived on the reservation since I graduated from high school. They may assert that I don't belong anymore, and so, consequently, this is not my story to tell. Some tribal members may see this book as a betrayal because it represents a dark time in Colville history, but I hope they come to celebrate the strength and vision of actors on both sides of the debate, as I have.

Learning about termination was bracing; learning about my community's role in the termination debate was a shock. I was proud of the community's active role in negotiating on behalf of or against the policy and of the proponents' pursuit of their legal rights ascribed by the government. But I was horrified to realize that we could have lost everything— and become homeless and nameless—because those same people were tired of the BIA. The tenacity exhibited on both sides of the termination debate on the Colville Reservation was remarkable, and that is the story I want readers to learn and appreciate. Both sides negotiated with the government in ever more sophisticated ways. Both felt vindicated by being on the "right" side. Both celebrated the individuality of the tribal bands. They debated on the reservation, in Spokane and Seattle, and in Washington, DC, making their arguments and pleading their cases, and they refused to be ignored.

When the National Congress of American Indians (NCAI) told the Colvilles that they were putting Indian country in peril, the Colvilles told them to mind their own business. It was a reasonable response from one tribe to the others. Native scholarship and scholarship about Natives during the last decades have reinforced assertions that disagreement among tribal communities does not reduce the weight of our words or the importance of our goals. Factionalism can be bad for communities, but I refuse to give that word power over the Colvilles when outsiders— be they scholars or members of other tribes—use it as a theoretical critique of our identity.

Many tribal members were dismayed by the choice of the seated tribal council to withdraw from NCAI and the Affiliated Tribes of Northwest Indians (ATNI), but it is also fair to say that those organizations abandoned the anti-termination Colvilles even as they fought the pro-termination groups. Because the Colvilles could not agree, the external groups could not determine how to work with tribal members outside the structure of the tribal council, and ultimately the NCAI and ATNI provided little aid in the termination battles.

Can I imagine our current tribal council telling other tribes to mind their own business today? Not really. Our tribal government and its representatives have grown apace with Indian and national politics, and our government enacted more formalized approaches to governance during and because of the termination era. We collaborate well with our neighbors and cousins on the Yakama, Spokane, and Coeur d'Alene reservations, just to name a few, and we have continuous relationships with politicians in state and federal governments. But would it be acceptable for our tribal council to tell others to back off? I think so.

As illuminating and challenging as learning about my community's history proved to be, I still approach this work with a tremendous sense of pride in and appreciation for the efforts tribal members on both sides made to be heard. That is why the tribal council's consistent refusal to let me use our tribal archives for this history is confusing. Colville tribal members were so engaged with this topic that our tribal newspaper, the *Tribal Tribune*, was created to keep people informed, and a second newspaper, *Our Heritage*, was created in pursuit of balanced reporting. The federal records are rich with tribal members' testimonies at hearings, as well as letters to senators, congressmen, and four presidents. Lucy Covington, an important leader during and after the termination era, left her papers to the tribe, as did Frank George, another anti-terminationist. There are undoubtedly valuable photos and letters in their collections in the tribal archives, but I may never know, because the council controls access. I wholly endorse the tribe's right to limit outsider access to tribal archives, but as a tribal member, I feel that those histories belong to all of us.

Writing this history has been possible because of the sources I found elsewhere. Tribal members' voices resonate through their official testimonies and their letters, and a wealth of documents related to Colville termination is available at the National Archives and Records Administration Pacific Alaska Region (Seattle); the National Archives and Records Administration in Washington, DC; the Smithsonian's National Museum of the American Indian Archives in Suitland, Maryland; the Manuscripts, Archives, and Special Collections (MASC) in Washington State University's Holland and Terrell Library; and the Spokane Public Library's Special Collections. Great material on the early Colville Reservation period resides in the Edward E. Ayer Collection at the Newberry Library. When community members testified at the hearings, they sometimes included their band affiliation as well as their names. I included those confirmed affiliations throughout this work, but in places where tribal members did not identify their band membership, I used only their names.

I did not conduct any oral histories for this research, because termination is relatively recent and still painful. In the casual conversations I had with folks at home about this project, responses ranged from "We didn't do that, right?" to "We're almost broke anyway, which is like slow termination." Mostly, the people I talked to about that time remembered the discussions but didn't want to relive them.

Like many tribal stories, this one is about an event. The Colvilles' quest to restore the lands of the lost North Half of the reservation resulted in a bargain, the land in exchange for termination, and this bargain initiated one long tribal skirmish over termination. Implicitly, then, this is a tribal narrative of what happened, and what happened next. Time is what moves this story forward, because the event can only be understood chronologically. That is how you will read it here, and you will learn the story of Colville termination as I did, through tribal members' words.

ACKNOWLEDGMENTS

This project has been both professionally and personally rewarding for me. Professionally, I have followed in the footsteps of the discipline's leading scholars through my research at the National Archives and Records Administration in Seattle and in Washington, DC; at the National Museum of the American Indian Archives in Suitland, Maryland; and at the Edward E. Ayer Collection at the Newberry Library in Chicago.

The Frances C. Allen Fellowship at the Newberry Library introduced me to the D'Arcy McNickle Center and the fine Newberry resources, and documents in the Ayer collection have allowed me to develop a deeper understanding of the early Colville Reservation. I am particularly proud to be a member of the Allen Fellowship cohort, because the fellowship has funded the scholarship of Native women for a generation and because it introduced me to the late Helen Hornbeck Tanner. Helen's observations on this project and on the scholar's role in telling Native American history have stayed with me since those fellowship years, and I am happy that I'll always be able to draw on them. Robert Galler was director of the D'Arcy McNickle Center then, and our informal conversations during my fellowship period would come in immensely handy when I accepted the assistant director position at the McNickle Center during Brian Hosmer's era as director. I met so many great people through the McNickle Center, both Native scholars and Native community leaders, and I am pleased to call so many of them friends.

Speaking of friends, a number of senior colleagues at Arizona State University offered great insight and critiques on my work on termination. I especially thank Peter Iverson, Robert Trennert, and Matthew Whitaker, as well as Kyle Longley and Rachel Fuchs. Brian Collier and Melody Miyamoto offered both fellowship and friendship; I thank them for it here and celebrate it every day. Peter Blodgett at the Huntington

Library has been a font of information and a cheerleader at the moments I needed one most. I'm so happy that he adopted the Tempe Trio and continues to indulge our collective calamity. Thanks to Amy Lonetree for many thoughtful conversations about scholarship and the discipline, and for the tips on productivity. They all made a big difference.

My Chicago pals deserve thanks for their support and patience while I researched and completed this project. Liz Hassel and Shawn-Laree de St. Aubin helped me to see the story from the outside again, and their questions improved the book. Their friendships enrich my life, and each of them is a beacon reminding me that Chicago is home, too.

The Institute for Scholarship in the Liberal Arts (ISLA) in the College of Arts and Letters at the University of Notre Dame has supported this project financially while also encouraging me to grow intellectually through engagement with my field and my peers. Ruth Abbey, former ISLA director, read some pieces of this project and offered terrific insight. Thanks to Harriet Baldwin, Pat Base, Agustin Fuentes, Ken Garcia, and Lauri Roberts in ISLA for their support while I put the finishing touches on the manuscript.

Julidta Tarver first expressed interest in this project before her retirement from University of Washington Press, and Marianne Keddington-Lang gamely took the project on in its early days. Marianne has been a great and patient shepherd; I so appreciate everything she has contributed to this project. Julidta's and Marianne's interest is even more rewarding because they are longtime friends of my undergraduate mentor, William G. Robbins. Bill also read bits and pieces of this project, and I was so glad to have his insights. Thank you to Kerrie Maynes and Marilyn Trueblood at the University of Washington Press. The close eye they lent the manuscript tightened those final few details and gave form to the book. Big thanks also go out to Thomas Eykemans of the Press for making the book look so great and for using all of the photographs! I also appreciate Alice Herbig and Rachael Levay for their assistance in publicizing and marketing the book. It's amazing to review the great number of resources that went into creation of one book. Staff at both NARA locations; at NMAI Suitland; at the Newberry Library (thanks to John Aubrey, Autumn Mather, and Jill Gage); at the Manuscripts, Archives, and Special Collections (MASC) in Washington State University's Holland and Terrell Library; and at the Spokane Public Library's Special Collections provided amazing assistance throughout this project. Archivists and librarians are wonderful people, that's all there is to it! Financial support from the Frances C. Allen Fellowship, from the Phillips Fund for Native American Research at the American Philosophical Society, and from the Kennedy Library Foundation Schwartz Research Fellowship moved this project forward at critical moments, and I thank all of the donors who made this funding possible.

Finally, thank you to my parents for giving me a life on the reservation and for always encouraging me to see the world beyond its borders.

BARTERING
WITH THE BONES
OF THEIR DEAD

LANDSCAPE EAST OF NESPELEM

CHAPTER 1

"We want to be Indians forever."

THIS story begins with the land. The Columbia Plateau served as home to bands of indigenous peoples long before the US government existed and even longer before that government named some of these peoples the Colville Indians. The plateau, roughly bounded by the Columbia River and the Cascade Mountain range in present-day Washington State, sheltered and sustained generations of people. Some of this plateau would be set aside for the Colville Indian Reservation in 1872, and, twenty short years later, more than one million acres of the North Half of the reservation would be lost to the very government that had deemed it reservation land in the first place. Loss of this land, through a questionable land cession, in many ways defined the Colville Indian Tribe throughout most of the twentieth century. In hopes of restoring the North Half to the reservation, the Colvilles engaged with several federal Indian policies. They accepted allotment. They rejected the Indian Reorganization Act (IRA) but then created a tribal constitution and empowered a business council to act on tribal matters. One of the Colville Business Council's first major undertakings in the early 1950s was preparation of legislation to restore the beloved North Half of the Colville Reservation. What began as a restoration bill became a bill providing for both restoration and termination, which ultimately led to a series of termination bills written by the Colville Business Council and by various factions on the reservation.

The yearning, the acrimony, the bitterness, and the discord that took

3

hold of the Colville Reservation and tribal members across the country for twenty years began with a good deed. Like most tribal communities, the Colvilles have a complicated land history and an even more complicated relationship with the government. The reservation was established by an executive order from President Ulysses S. Grant in 1872, the government's attempt at an efficient solution for dealing with the eight bands of non-treaty Indians that the reservation would include. The first executive order, signed in April, created a reservation that spanned roughly 3.5 million acres on both sides of the Columbia River all the way to the Pend Oreille River near present-day Idaho, and included white settlement areas near Kettle Falls and Colville, Washington. After howls of protest from non-Indian mill operators and shopkeepers who had arrived in the area not long before, President Grant adjusted the reservation boundary to the west side of the Columbia River, thus leaving the townsfolk outside the reservation.[1]

The new reservation encompassed 3.1 million acres, from the Canadian border on the north and following the jogs and turns of the Columbia River for its eastern and southern boundaries. The western boundary had less physical or territorial finality to it, but it ran along streams and lakes, and nearly reached the foothills of the Cascade range. The Colville Indian Reservation became home to the newly anointed Colville Indians circa July 1872.[2]

This new collective seemed to barely acknowledge their new name. The Colville band lived closest to the white settlements and had well-established trade relationships with Hudson's Bay Company (HBC) in Canada.[3] This new designation required them to make few changes; they kept their name and stayed in nearly the same places, so at the time they likely felt little effect from the executive order. The Arrow Lakes band (also called the Lakes band), the nearest neighbor of the Colville band, were canoe people who fished and hunted along the Columbia on both sides of the US-Canadian border, and it is likely that they just kept about their business. The Lakes band also had longstanding trade relationships with HBC men and sometimes married these traders as well. Consequently each group had integrated non-Indians into their lives as much or as little as they individually deemed necessary.

The San Poil Indians, farther down the Columbia near what is now Keller, almost completely ignored the government men and other outsiders. They did not trade with whites, did not engage in Catholicism as did some in the Colville band, and kept to themselves in an area rich with game and fish.[4] The most interior of the bands, they would rebuff government overtures well into the twentieth century.

The Nespelem band and the Okanogan band also remained in their usual areas, along the southwestern and northwestern edges of the new reservation, because the executive order included land they already considered home. The Okanogans traveled to and from Canada frequently, where they too enjoyed a good trade relationship with HBC.[5]

The Okanogans and the Nespelems historically had the most frequent contact with the neighboring bands of Indians who were now considered part of the Colville Indian Tribe and who would slowly begin to make their homes on the Colville Reservation. The Chelan, Entiat, and Methow bands had lived west and south of the Colville Reservation. These bands engaged in trade and intermarriage with some of the Colville bands, but had likely not considered themselves linked with the Colvilles in any more formal way. But because all eight bands were non-treaty Indians, and because the government wanted to formalize boundaries and land agreements, they all became Colville Indians.

Two later additions to the Colville Indian Reservation caused a stir among the existing tribal members. In 1884 the Moses band of Columbia Indians joined the residents of the Colville Reservation, a move coordinated by the US government without consulting the Colvilles.[6] One year later Moses invited Chief Joseph, newly released from prison, and his band of Nez Perce Indians to reside on the Colville Reservation as well. Joseph, by some accounts Moses's cousin, had led a band of roughly 700 Nez Perce from their home in the Wallowa Valley of Oregon toward the Canadian border in flight from the US cavalry and in defiance of orders to move to the new Nez Perce Reservation in Idaho. Nez Perce territory had cut a broad swath across present-day southeastern Washington, northeastern Oregon, and central Idaho. As white settlement expanded in Washington Territory in the 1850s, the US government sought to secure more land for settlers, and convinced the Nez Perce leaders to sign a treaty in 1855 setting aside nearly eight million acres as the Nez Perce Reservation but reducing the traditional Nez Perce land base.

Upon the heels of a gold rush, less than ten years later, the United States offered another treaty, shrinking the Nez Perce Reservation to fewer than one million acres and offering a hospital as well as financial compensation in return. Chief Joseph's father, Joseph the Elder, refused to sign this new treaty, and his band became a band of non-treaty Indians. The treaty bands settled on the Nez Perce Reservation in present-day Lapwai, Idaho, and the non-treaty bands stayed in the Wallowa Valley, a decision that ultimately led to Joseph's flight. When Joseph finally surrendered in the fall of 1877 after three months of evading the cavalry, he and his remaining followers were taken to Fort Leavenworth prison in Kansas, then were settled in Indian Territory in Oklahoma for ten years. Upon their release, Joseph's band of non-treaty Nez Perce, as this group came to be known, could not return to their former home in the Wallowa Valley of Oregon. Even after being returned from Indian Territory, Joseph's band did not want to reside on the Nez Perce Reservation. Chief Moses offered Joseph and his band a new home on Colville land, and Joseph accepted.

Local resentment flared, and still lingers, over these two additions to the reservation. The eight original bands of Colville Indians did not consider Moses a native of their region. To them, he was a guest. Many tribal members regarded Moses's invitation to Joseph a cultural faux pas. In 1965 one tribal member expressed a sentiment that still resonates with some tribal members:

> The Nez Perce were prisoners of war, and yet they were placed here on this reservation among us peaceful Colvilles. The Nez Perce fought the United States government, took many lives and cost the people a lot of money, but us Colvilles never fought the government—we was [sic] always peaceful. That's the way it still is today with them; trying always to get control and take over the reservation for themselves.[7]

The Colvilles, put together on a reservation without a choice, resented the government for negotiating with Moses and Joseph, and for adding these two bands to their reservation. Moses at least had kinship ties, but the Nez Perce had been aggressors in the region, and it is likely that some Colville Indians still distrusted them.

Thirty years after the Colville Indian Reservation was established, the last two bands who would become Colville Indians, the Wenatchi and the Palus, arrived on the reservation. White settlement had pushed them from their homelands to the south. Many of their relations resided on the Colville Reservation, and they chose to join their kin rather than suffer the advancing encroachment.[8]

The original bands of the Colville land base—the Colvilles, the Lakes, the San Poil, the Nespelem, and the Okanogan, all Salish language speakers—had kinship and trade relationships with one another, and, because of those ties, enjoyed loyalty shared among friends. Loyalty cannot be interpreted as unity, however. None of the bands could have anticipated the government's expectation that they cooperate as one group. Nor would they have imagined that the US government would force them to accept as neighbors the Nez Perce, a band of Indians who spoke a different language (Sahaptian) and who had acted combatively against smaller Indian bands as well as against the United States and some of its citizens. Despite being compressed onto one reservation, the bands would always maintain much of their individual identities. Each band listened to its own leaders, and, while the leaders may have cooperated across bands to interpret the motives of non-Indians, for example, each still advanced his own method for dealing with white neighbors. This sense of band identification and ongoing questions about how to define themselves as "Colville Indians" would have a tremendous impact on the termination debates of the 1960s.

The years following the establishment of the new reservation brought more attention from the government and more oversight of tribal lives and lifestyles. The new Indian agent, who arrived near the town of Colville shortly after the reservation was established, encouraged farming and cultivation rather than subsistence on hunting, fishing, and digging roots.[9] Many Colvilles were reluctant to engage heavily in these practices or to rely on farming exclusively and continued some of their previous migratory practices as the seasons changed. Consequently, the Indian agent and the territorial governor reported that the Colvilles were not using the land.

It was, of course, a false statement. Members of the Colville bands hunted and fished across their homeland. They gathered roots and tart huckleberries from hidden spots near summer campgrounds at higher elevations. They traversed the land to find what they needed, and could trade with neighboring tribes if their homeland (or the agent) could not provide all they sought. The land and the rivers and the lakes of the Colville Reservation sustained the band members. Despite the tribal members' broad uses of the land and their cultural connection it, the difference in the interpretation of land "use" between the Indians and the government led to the single most distressing event in Colville history: the loss of the North Half.

In 1891 the government began negotiations with the Colville Indians to buy 1.5 million acres of the north half of the reservation (the North Half) and open it for settlement by the turn of the century. The House Committee on Indian Affairs deemed the reservation's vastness "no less an injustice to the Indians themselves than a menace to the progress of the surrounding commonwealth." The committee determined that the Colvilles could learn only from the "well-ordered white communities" that would surround them, and that the Colvilles could begin to embrace and profit from new market economies that would emerge in response to the newcomers' needs. Congress agreed to pay 1.5 million dollars, one dollar per acre, for the land. An elder member of the tribe brought up the disputed land sale during discussions about termination and reminded tribal members of previous broken promises, "It was no more than a land steal and some of our teen-age boys were allowed to sign the so-called agreement between the Indians and the government."[10]

Bills approving the sale of the North Half to the United States repeatedly died in congressional sessions, and fifteen years elapsed before Congress ratified the purchase agreement, but the North Half still opened for settlement as scheduled in 1900. A scandal erupted in 1904 when it came to light that a former Indian agent, A. M. Anderson, had coerced Colville chief Barnaby to participate in a scam to secure money from the Colvilles. Fired by President Theodore Roosevelt in 1902 for bribery, perjury, and forgery of an annuity payroll on the Coeur d'Alene Reservation, Anderson induced Barnaby to sign a contract indicating he had power of attorney for 131 Colville tribal members. Anderson, as their broker, promised he would arrange payment for the North Half from Washington, and in exchange would take a ten-percent fee from the Indians. When questioned about it later, Barnaby explained that he had not read the contract, nor had it been translated for him, and that he had acted only on his own account, not for other Indians. He said he told tribal members what he had done when he returned home from seeing Anderson and that they had expressed little interest.[11]

Despite Anderson's alleged connections in Washington, DC, he returned empty-handed. Many Indians would have rejected a payment anyway because they refused to give credence to the "land steal" perpetrated by the government. In 1906 in a letter to the Department of Justice, agent John McAdams Webster characterized the San Poil band in particular as being aloof from government interference:

> They have always refused to enter into any agreement in regard to the disposition or sale of their lands; refused to be bound by the Government or other tribes who they regard as interlopers on their lands and they have consistently held to this. They announced then as they have always done that if the entire million and a half dollars were piled on the floor in front of them and they were told to help themselves not a penny of it would they accept. They stoutly claim ownership of the lands on which they have lived for generations and would not sell for any price but acknowledge the right of other tribes to barter with the graves and bones of their dead.[12]

By 1905, however, some of the bands grew progressively more frustrated at living with white encroachment while still being impoverished. Indians grew weary of seeing whites settle on good hunting lands and block good fishing areas. They witnessed white settlers receiving consideration from local and federal governments while Indians were punished for trespassing on lands that had always belonged to them. Major James McLaughlin, an Indian inspector, finally spent several weeks with the Colvilles at the end of that year to arrange for allotment of the South Half of the reservation and soothe tempers about the uncompensated loss of the North Half. Some Colvilles viewed McLaughlin's timing as manipulative, because he arrived at the coldest time of year, when most people stayed close to home, and he expected all of the Colvilles to travel to meet with him. This perceived power play created much bitterness and resentment. The policy of allotment emerged from the Dawes Act in 1887 and provided for individual Indian ownership of land in order to move away from collective tribal ownership of lands. The policy was designed to decrease collective tribal identities, which reformers believed would lead to increased Indian assimilation into the white culture, and also to remove land from tribal ownership and place it into the for-profit real estate market. Allotment impacted Indians and Indian land bases throughout the United States.[13]

In the course of allotment talks with the Colvilles, McLaughlin reassured the Colvilles that the government would honor allotment agreements for the South Half and would protect them from non-Indian encroachment until the allotment process had been completed. He also gave his word that once the Colvilles agreed to the South Half allotment, they would be paid for the ceded North Half as promised in 1891.[14] One of those reassurances proved to be a promise he could not keep. When Congress finally passed the Colville Diminishment Act in 1906, the act that provided for purchase of the North Half, it did secure the reservation along its current 1.4-million-acre boundary. However, Congress refused a payout for the North Half lands. Instead, the act mandated that proceeds from allotments on the North Half sold to non-Indians would go into a government fund for "the education and civilization" of the Colville Indians. Those proceeds never made it into Colville coffers, and the Colvilles have as of yet received no compensation for the North Half.

The Colville Indians' collective experience with the federal government is not unique—for example, executive order reservations were created in Washington, Idaho, Colorado, Utah, and Arizona, and many tribal confederations grew out of several disparate indigenous communities being moved on to one land base—but it does have exceptional aspects. Because the bands did not present a threat to white settlement or to peace, the territorial and federal governments were able to put off dealing with them until late in the nineteenth century. In contrast to the first removal of Native Americans from their traditional homelands, which officially began under president Andrew Jackson in 1830, the bands of the Colville Indians enjoyed decades of relative tranquility from settler-related issues and associated political initiatives.

The Colville Indians also sidestepped the Dawes Act for two decades after its inception. While the North Half cession was pursued as part of the overall allotment program begun in 1877, the Colvilles did not face allotment on the South Half of the reservation until after the turn of the twentieth century.

The Colville Indians' rejection of the Indian Reorganization Act (IRA) in 1936 represents another unique aspect of the tribe's experience with federal Indian policy. The IRA provided for creation of a local tribal government that would be largely free of federal government interference; called for the federal government to more actively train Native Americans for employment, including employment within the Office of Indian Affairs (which became the Bureau of Indian Affairs in 1947); ended further allotment of Indian lands; and created a Court of Indian Affairs to adjudicate matters related to Native Americans more fairly and sympathetically than non-Indian courts could. All of this was also supposed to be accomplished while integrating individual tribal values and cultural practices. The Colvilles rejected the act and the constitution that the Interior Department had drafted for them, while many other tribes chose to engage with the IRA.[15] Some tribal members rejected the act because they trusted the leadership of their band chiefs or headmen and wanted to maintain that political structure. Others rejected it because they did not feel that band members had enough education to manage the reservation or to follow the laws and rules that the IRA would require. Some favored the IRA because they wanted to end Office of Indian Affairs (OIA) control of tribal matters and instead favored the creation of formal band governments within the Colville Indian Reservation.

At this time, a group of tribal members on the reservation formed the Colville Indian Association (CIA). The CIA wanted a tribal government that provided elected participatory political leadership from each district. Members of the CIA felt that neither the chiefs nor the OIA did enough for the Colvilles' interests, and the group embraced the IRA as a solution to both complaints.[16] Ultimately, the Colville-designed constitution provided for that exact kind of tribal government structure: officials elected from each district on the reservation, according to the population of the district. The Colville Indian Association had an active membership during the 1930s but fell dormant after the confederation became enacted. Tribal members revived it during the termination era, still calling it CIA, as a group in support of termination. Their position on termination was consistent with the original group's efforts to be free of the OIA.[17]

Although the Colville Indians rejected the IRA, they ultimately wrote a constitution of their own, based on other IRA constitutions, and became the Colville Confederated Tribes on February 26, 1938. In forming a confederation, the twelve bands of the Colville Tribes ceded their power to act or govern as individual bands to the tribal institution. This institutionalization of power represents a major cultural and political step away from traditional band governing, which was usually implemented by elected chiefs after reaching community consensus. A central tribal government populated by tribal members from each district and making decisions based on majority opinions was a dramatic shift, and during the termination debates, many tribal members would assert their desire to terminate the Colville tribal confederation in favor of a return to traditional band leadership.

The Colvilles created several drafts before they produced a constitution supported by the BIA and tolerated by the Colville constitutional committee. Only one-third of the 1,746 eligible voters—men and women enrolled in the tribe and over twenty-one years old—participated in the election to accept the constitution; in a vote of 503 to 79, the Colvilles approved the constitution that still governs them today. More than 1,100 tribal members eligible to vote voiced their silent opposition to the matter by declining to participate. Refusal to participate in elections as a form of protest is still a common practice. Months after the vote, a few tribal members wrote to President Franklin D. Roosevelt and indicated their displeasure with the new tribal government and tribal representatives. They did not trust these newly elected officials. "We have leaders or Chiefs in our own districts. . . . We want our old laws; we want to be Indians forever."[18]

The tribal council, a body first created by Commissioner John Collier and then legislatively empowered by the Colville constitution, emerged as the governing body of the reservation. Elected by tribal members in each of the four districts—Omak, Nespelem, Keller, and Inchelium—the council met only a few times a year at Nespelem during the first two decades of governance.[19] In the late 1950s, the council organized a small tribal government staff, housed in the BIA agency at Nespelem, and became a more formal body.[20]

As the twentieth century wore on, the loss of the North Half remained painful for the Colville tribal members. Almost as soon as the Indian Claims Commission was established in 1946, the Colville Business Council filed a bill for the restoration of the North Half.[21] In 1934 and 1935, secretary of the Interior Harold Ickes had issued departmental orders withdrawing 818,000 acres of unalloted land on the North Half from further disposition until the matter of compensation and ownership was resolved.[22] The government clearly recognized an obligation in this matter, even though the parties could not agree on what that obligation entailed.

While awaiting review of the ICC claim, the Colville Business Council also approached Congressman Walt Horan about coauthoring a congressional bill to restore the unalloted lands of the former North Half of the reservation to the Colville Tribes.[23] From 1943 to 1965 Horan, who had had lifelong exposure to Native land issues in the Columbia Plateau region, served as US representative for Washington's fifth district, which encompasses most of Eastern Washington. It is evident from business council meeting transcripts and from correspondence with BIA, Department of the Interior, and other officials that by the early 1950s the business council felt comfortable with Horan and believed he would assist them with restoration of the North Half. This dialogue was well developed by 1953, when the topic of termination tied to restoration first emerged. Horan discussed termination as an option for the Colville Tribes even before the first termination bill was signed into law.[24]

By October 1953 the business council had embraced the notion of termination and was prepared to end the Colville Confederated Tribes' relationship with the federal government and eliminate the federal tribal designation. They requested a meeting with the new commissioner of Indian Affairs, Glenn Emmons, during his visit to the Yakama Reservation. Many tribal governments had high hopes for Emmons; he was a banker from Gallup, New Mexico, who had the strong support of the Navajos. Consequently, the Colville Business Council traveled 180 miles on two-lane roads to south central Washington State to make a thirty-minute presentation, anticipating that Emmons would engage with them on termination and help them find a solution. Indian communities across the United States had hoped to have some input on who would assume the role of commissioner once the divisive Dillon S. Myer had been dismissed from that office. Indians hoped to see an Indian in that role, and many tribes put forth candidates, but Emmons ultimately won the office. Indians were optimistic about him because of his work with the Navajos, many of whom respected him, but as a finance-centered person, he favored private property and fiscal independence and embraced the charge for termination with some enthusiasm. Still, councilman John Cleveland presented the Colville case:

> We sincerely realize that the time has come for us to start planning for
> the final withdrawal of Government supervision. . . . We are exploring
> the feasibility of developing an appropriate over-all program for the
> Colville Indians contemplating our release from Federal supervision.
> It is our desire to enjoy and have the same rights and responsibilities
> as all other American citizens. We sincerely hope that you will show
> a sympathetic understanding of the problems which face our Indian

people and work toward their final solution so that we may exercise the full prerogatives of American citizenship. . . . We will work and plan for the day when all of our Indian citizens will come into their rightful heritage of full freedom and responsibility.[25]

Cleveland's language, on behalf of the council, clearly mirrored the language of House Concurrent Resolution 108:

Whereas it is the policy of Congress, as rapidly as possible, to make the Indians within the territorial limits of the United States subject to the same laws and entitled to the same responsibilities as are applicable to other citizens of the United States and to grant them all of the rights and prerogatives pertaining to American citizenship; and Whereas the Indians within the territorial limits of the United States should assume their full responsibilities as American citizens.[26]

The Colville Business Council, certainly with Horan's assistance, had done their homework before meeting with Emmons. Not only did they employ identical language in their presentation but they also secured support for the restoration bill from the boards of county commissioners in Ferry and Okanogan counties (the two reservation counties), the Washington State Association of County Commissioners, the Okanogan Valley Chamber of Commerce, and "other responsible groups interested in the future welfare of the Colville Indians."

While acknowledging that federal withdrawal was inevitable, the council also wanted to hold Emmons accountable. Cleveland indicated that the tribe expected technical help from professionals to assess land and mineral values and to calculate the costs associated with health and education benefits provided to Colville tribal members as they prepared their withdrawal plan and tried to prepare for the future.[27]

Emmons knew little about the Colvilles or their situation going into the meeting, and he did not know how the reservation was formed. He asked a few questions during the presentation but remained noncommittal, although he did praise the business council for recognizing that a withdrawal plan would be necessary in the near future.

Barely two months after the passage of House Concurrent Resolution 108 (H.C.R. 108), the Colville Business Council actively engaged the Interior Department and other officials to discuss their options for termination. The council recognized the importance of preparation in advance of creating a termination plan and submitting legislation to achieve the twin goals of restoration and termination. The Colville Tribes were not among the tribes targeted for termination by H.C.R. 108, and they were the only tribe to request termination in exchange for a land restoration.[28] The Colvilles were not the only tribe who favored termination, however. In 1951 the Confederated Tribes of Siletz Indians of Oregon passed a council resolution to terminate the federal trust relationship, largely because community members and the tribal organization were frustrated with federal management of their affairs—also a common theme throughout Colville termination discussions. Siletz support of termination would eventually lead to termination of "the western tribes of Oregon," as they were classed by Congress, including many smaller groups, such as the Coos, the Lower Umpqua, and the Siuslaw, who did not favor termination at all.[29]

The fact that the Colvilles pursued termination without pressure from the US government creates even more of an impetus to understand how and why the quest for and the battle against termination lasted so long. Factionalism within the tribe, and even within the tribal council, energized the debate. Throughout the Colville termination era, from 1953 to 1972, four to six factions for and against termination operated at any given time.[30] Factions within the pro-termination camp disagreed on the length of time until withdrawal, on the amount of compensation tribal members should expect, and on the language in various termination bills, but all acted as proponents of termination. The Petitioners Party began as a compromise group—they acknowledged that termination might be inevitable but proposed alternative solutions that would protect the land base and tribal members who wished to retain their federal recognition. Within a year of their founding, however, they became strict anti-terminationists and aligned with other anti-terminationists to fight the policy without division.

While factionalism created schisms that in some cases still exist, fervent disagreement and refusal to compromise on the withdrawal process are ultimately what saved the Colvilles from termination. The testimonies at the Colville termination hearings throughout the 1960s illustrated a lack of unity on the concept and practice of termination, which gave BIA and Interior Department officials pause and caused concern among some members of Congress. The hearings' publications also reflect official concern over language in the Colville termination bills, especially concerning voting requirements, which favored the passage of termination by a majority of tribal members voting, rather than a majority of members eligible to vote. The votes to terminate the mixed-blood Utes in Utah and the Klamath Tribe in Oregon were passed by a majority of members voting rather than a tribal majority, and BIA officials quickly comprehended the inherent flaws of that practice. Whether federal government officials understood the cultural implications of nonparticipation in a vote as condemnation of the issue being decided is not clear, but the BIA administrators did recognize that implementing dramatic termination legislation on the advice of a small number of Colville tribal members would create another problematic situation for the bureau at Colville. The BIA refused to endorse any bill containing such a limited voting requirement.[31]

The first pro-termination faction emerged shortly after the business council's meeting with Emmons in October 1953. The Colville Commercial Club, also called the Nespelem Indian Commercial Club, promoted the immediate restoration of the North Half followed by the immediate termination of the Colville Reservation, in hopes of making a lucrative financial deal and gaining economically from the distribution of tribal assets. Commercial Club members had long been frustrated by restrictions on timber sales and grazing leases imposed by the BIA, and likely saw restoration and termination as a way to regain control.[32]

Given the somewhat informal structure of the tribal entity at that time, and considering that only a minority of tribal members had home telephones in the early 1950s, this early faction is quite remarkable. The business council began planning a series of meetings across the four districts to discuss restoration and termination, but no official meetings about these two possibilities occurred before 1954. Therefore, the Colville Commercial Club (CCC) made a point of investigating the law and the termination options on their own initiative. While the CCC was the first organized group to research termination options, later groups would be just as organized in their approach, and some of them would effectively employ public relations strategies and leverage non-Indian elected officials to their own advantage.

Because the Columbia Plateau is so remote, it is tempting to assume that the Colville Indians might have been unsophisticated or that they lacked exposure to political practices. Few tribal members had gone to college at that time, and although some had served in the military or attended boarding schools and then returned, many reservation residents had not lived away from the reservation. Certainly some tribal members approached termination from an emotional perspective rather than a practical one—this is especially true of termination opponents who did not want to lose their homes. But just as many community members opposed termination because they understood that the government had a responsibility to them. The government designated the Colville Confederated Tribes as inherently sovereign, empowered to govern as a tribe, and the US government had to honor and protect the sovereignty it legitimized when it created the Colville Reservation. Of those who favored termination, some employed arguments that also asserted sovereignty as the right to be free of BIA rules and interference.[33]

Desire for sovereignty and freedom motivated both sides of the termination debate, and tribal members on both sides of the issue struggled with questions of identity and what it meant to be a Colville Indian. While some divisions along band lines occurred, either in favor of termination or against, it would be an oversimplification to assess the Colville termination debate as a battle of the bands. General lines of support and opposition can also be traced along reservation and off-reservation populations, in terms of youth and age, and according to blood quantum, but many tribal members crossed these lines of demarcation, so a general conclusion regarding one population supporting one position on termination would be false.

As the Colville Business Council began more formal conversations about the North Half land bill and the possibility of withdrawal, they also immediately indicated that they expected performance from the government agencies engaged in these conversations. One week after the council met with Commissioner Emmons in October 1953, the congressional Committee on Interior and Insular Affairs visited Nespelem, the seat of the Colville Agency. At that meeting, the council indicated that it hoped to continue operating the reservation under the constitution currently in place, with the trusteeship responsibility remaining with the federal government. The council also asserted that it needed the committee to assist with early passage of the land restoration bill related to the North Half, and that during the approvals process of that bill, the council would "sit down at a conference table and discuss and plan for the future welfare of our people." Council members wanted the tribe to be free to manage their own affairs and make their own decisions. In the same meeting, tribal council chairman James White told the congressional committee that the council recognized that, even though they hoped to retain federal trusteeship status, withdrawal of trusteeship seemed a foregone conclusion. Consequently, the council hoped the committee would support the Colvilles remaining under federal trusteeship for the maximum length of time, until the tribe had become prepared to operate a successful corporation.[34]

One of the first tribal membership meetings about restoration and withdrawal produced mixed reactions to the council's plan for restoration followed by termination. The council had invited the three eldest tribal leaders to speak at the meeting: Chief Jim James, Billy Curlew, and Peter Dan Moses. The leaders indicated that the people unanimously supported restoration but that many wanted to retain trustee status. Chief Jim James, a leader of the San Poil band, stated that "the majority of the people feel that the government has benefited the people more than what they otherwise would have received from any other source." He also reported that some people, likely other tribal members, had offered him money to sign a petition for termination, but asserted that he had not signed and probably never would.[35] Billy Curlew and Peter Dan Moses, leaders of the Moses-Columbia band, echoed James's assessment. While James's statement about the government being good for the Indians may seem strange coming from the leader of the San Poil band, the band that agent John McAdams Webster had characterized as aloof to US government priorities, it can also be understood as promoting the status quo. Termination of federal supervision would mean tumult for the tribal members, including loss of land. After witnessing the changes that other governmental policies had wrought, James perhaps believed that the Colville people would fare better under the current system. Congressman Walt Horan also attended this meeting, and responded to James with an assurance that he was trying to protect Indian rights and believed that all treaties should be honored.[36]

Before delving further into the Colville termination story, it is important to note how wildly different the Colville process was from every other termination discussion. Many tribes ended up tied to termination because of receipt of a judgment or claim from the Indian Claims

Commission (ICC) or from Congress. Tribes could bring a claim against the United States through the ICC and receive monetary compensation for territory lost as a result of broken treaties or other agreements. The Bureau of Indian Affairs coerced the Menominee, Klamath, and Ute tribes to terminate because each had won a multimillion-dollar judgment, and the BIA asserted that the financial compensation would provide a good foundation for self-management. Tribes who did receive a claim award consistently wanted per capita payments as part of the judgment disbursement. Tribal members within those communities sought individual payments from these awards, and in most cases tribal leaders agreed that awards should be divided between building tribal infrastructure and creating per capita payments. Many members of Congress during this period saw tribal plans for per capita payouts as a waste of money. The dominant opinion held that tribal members would only spend the money, rather than invest it, so it remained the responsibility of the BIA and Congress to assist tribes in making plans for economic development. Officials viewed termination as a tool for economic development, because tribes would be free to plan and manage their own business affairs, rather than being supervised by the BIA. This justification was used repeatedly to put off payment of judgment awards until tribes had written termination legislation.

No other tribe tried to tie a claim to termination, however, like the Colvilles hoped to do. Where other tribes fought termination and strove to retain federal recognition, some Colvilles accepted—with alarming alacrity—termination as inevitable not just for their tribe but for all tribes. The business council accepted the loss of trustee status but welcomed the deal so long as the Colville Tribes regained the North Half as part of the bargain. Restoration of the land base that many tribal members believed had been unfairly taken from them overwhelmed the termination aspect of the land bill. Throughout Colville termination hearings in the 1960s, tribal members repeatedly asserted that they did not think they would really have to terminate, even after the restoration bill passed. So, while the business council seized an opportunity to regain the North Half, it is likely that tribal members were not fully engaged with the nuances of the termination requirement or likely that many believed that the Colville Tribes could renegotiate this agreement with the BIA.

Colville termination differed in other respects as well. The Klamath Tribe had almost no opportunity to review termination policy before that policy changed their lives, but the Colvilles, individually and collectively, studied and engaged with the policy for twenty years. The tribal newspaper, the *Tribal Tribune*, began as a forum for disseminating information on termination.[37] Lucy Covington, a tribal member and avid opponent of termination, started her own newspaper, *Our Heritage*, to offer tribal members an alternative to the *Tribune*. In it she outlined platforms of candidates running for tribal council who opposed termination.[38] The Colville Business Council and each of the pro-termination factions crafted termination legislation that would be introduced to Congress on their behalf. Other tribal groups targeted for termination pled for mercy from the policy, asserted that their people were not ready to live without trusteeship, and asked Congress to reconsider. The Colvilles' active pursuit of a policy that would destroy their nation is unlike any other, and the roots of this quest lie with the North Half.

However, what began as a struggle to regain lost land quickly became a struggle for control of the reservation. By the end of 1954, the Colville Indian Association had reemerged and had firmly established itself in opposition to the Colville Business Council to such an extent that Marcel Arcasa, president of the CIA, began communicating directly with senators Henry M. Jackson and George Malone of Washington State. The association passed resolutions related to tribal business, including timber management and health care, and clearly asserted itself as an alternative government on the reservation. When Senator Jackson forwarded one of these letters to the BIA, the commissioner of Indian Affairs responded by reminding Jackson that the CIA existed only as a faction on the reservation, and that the business council was the only body empowered to govern the Colvilles.[39]

The CIA led aggressively. They recruited new members through mailings and asserted that the Colville Business Council, the Affiliated Tribes of Northwest Indians (ATNI), and the National Congress of American Indians (NCAI) all falsely represented the Colville Indians. "In forming this organization, we are preparing for termination. . . . In order to take our place with the white man, we must wake up and fight. Through our organization . . . we can tell the world what we want and stand a chance of getting it and retaining it."[40] This group supported restoration of the North Half, but they felt that the tribal council planned to extend federal supervision for too long. The CIA wanted termination within three years of passage of a termination bill. They not only publicized their actions through mailings but also spoke to reporters at local and regional newspapers, and wrote letters to the editors.

The CIA and its members were sharply critical of the business council, and while they purported to represent the people of the Colville Tribes, the CIA disregarded those members who opposed termination. The year 1954 proved to be a hectic and divisive one on the Colville Reservation. In June of 1954 the business council held a general membership meeting to discuss restoration of the North Half and how that restoration bill would be tied to termination. At this meeting, three traditional band leaders spoke. Chief Jim James of the San Poils, Chief Victor Nicholas of the Lakes Band (Chief Barnaby's son), and Chief Cleveland Kamiakin of the Palus Band (and also from an important Yakama family) each opposed the bill. They did not support termination in principle but told tribal members that they feared termination to be inevitable. Congressman Horan attended the meeting as well and reinforced to the membership that he doubted that Congress would pass a bill that did not include some kind of termination provision tied to restoration.[41]

The Colvilles did draft a bill in 1954, but it did not advance through either house of Congress, and the business council returned to it in 1955. Because of all of the confusion surrounding the dual pursuit of restoration and termination, the business council struggled to create a workable plan. During a meeting at the Portland area office of the BIA in April 1955, the area director suggested that restoration and termination should be two separate bills, because one should not be dependent on the other. Don Foster, the director of the area office, recommended that the Colvilles take time to examine their restored land base in the context of the rest of the reservation before trying to create a plan for federal withdrawal. "We do not want another Klamath situation on our hands. [The Colvilles] must not make the same mistake the Klamaths did with a hasty termination bill."

At that same meeting, however, after learning from the Colvilles how strongly Horan believed Congress would not approve the restoration bill without some kind of termination clause, Foster wondered if the Colvilles could craft the bill to indicate that they would agree, within five years of restoration, to draft a plan for eventual termination. They would not have to terminate within five years, only to make a plan to terminate.[42]

Horan assisted the business council in drafting a bill for restoration and termination, following his own instincts based on feedback he had gotten from congressional peers. The council wrote a bill providing for the immediate restoration of the 818,000 acres. That bill included a promise from the Colvilles to draft a termination plan within five years of the land restoration. The bill also contained a stipulation, based on previous support from Ferry and Okanogan counties, that the two counties would receive $40,000 a year from the tribe as a form of payment for services (roads, public safety, and so on) until the tribe terminated. While the Colvilles debated restoration and termination among themselves, Native communities outside the reservation also weighed in on the proposed legislation. The Coeur d'Alene Indian Tribal Council unanimously signed a petition opposing the termination and county payment clauses of the Colville bill. While the Coeur d'Alenes, whose reservation is 100 miles from the Colville Reservation, wholeheartedly supported the Colvilles' quest for restoration of the unallotted lands on the North Half, they feared that the Colville restoration bill set two dangerous precedents: cash payments to counties for public services, and termination of federal supervision. The Coeur d'Alene council asserted to the Colvilles that the current friendly Congress would easily pass the restoration bill without termination attached, and encouraged the Colville Business Council to reconsider the bill. "With termination difficulties already experienced by some tribes, many Indian tribes stand ready to oppose your bill and will very likely defeat it." Coeur d'Alene chairman Lawrence Nicodemus urged the Colville council to revoke the $40,000 payment and amend the bill to remove termination as a requirement for the land restoration in order to represent a unified national Indian front: "There is nothing that would make our common enemy's work easier and more pleasant than for us to start Inter-tribal quarrels at this time."

Nicodemus went on to say that the NCAI, the ATNI, and the Inter-Tribal Council of Arizona, all would oppose the bill as it stood.[43] The chairman of the Colville Tribal Council, James D. White, responded strongly to Nicodemus, indicating that Nicodemus had not only interpreted the bill incorrectly but also that he did not belong in Colville tribal matters. "We have not, and so far as I am concerned, will not endeavor to shape the destiny of your tribe. We hope that you will be at least as considerate with respect to our efforts to determine the future of our tribe."[44]

White also wrote to Helen Peterson, executive director of the National

Congress of American Indians, urging her and the organization not to interfere with the Colville bill. Nicodemus had sent a copy of the Coeur d'Alene council's letter to the NCAI, and White shared his view of how the organization should respond to the situation: "We are counting on you and the NCAI to help us rather than to detract from our chances of at last getting the 818,000 acres back into tribal status."[45]

The NCAI and the Colvilles would be at odds to varying degrees after 1954, because the NCAI opposed Colville termination.[46] While the organization clearly supported the land restoration as the long-overdue fulfillment of a government promise, it did not endorse the terms of the compromise. The Colville Tribes had been a dues-paying member since the organization's founding in 1944, and many Colville tribal members had participated as leaders of the organization. This tussle over Colville restoration would inaugurate an era of decreasing support for Colville membership in the NCAI, and the council would eventually withdraw from the organization.[47]

The Colvilles won a Pyrrhic victory with the 1956 North Half land restoration. Upon passage of the bill Congressman Horan and the business council had crafted together, Public Law 772 (P.L. 772), the North Half lands were restored to the Colville Confederated Tribes, but the reservation boundaries were not adjusted. That land is still not included as part of the tribe's official landholdings. Instead, the tribe has rights to the land, such as hunting and fishing access, but the tribe does not own the land, and the reservation remains as it was in 1906 after cession of the North Half.[48]

After this in-name-only restoration of the unallotted lands on the North Half, which occurred a few months after the bill's passage in 1956, the business council spent the next several years drafting a plan for termination. While they considered termination, some council members believed that Congress would not really withdraw federal supervision, and that the Colvilles might both get to keep the North Half and retain trustee status.

This hope was reflected in the business council's lack of planning related to termination. Since the national mood was beginning to turn against termination, and since the NCAI and other tribal groups so ardently opposed the policy, the Colvilles likely hoped that Congress would bow to national pressures and repeal termination before their legislative deadline. That did not happen. Finally, in 1960, one year before the council was to submit a termination plan, the business council retained the Stanford Research Institute (SRI), the same firm hired by the Klamath Tribe and the BIA prior to that termination, to study possible withdrawal options. The SRI proposed three paths, all of which included living without federal supervision:

1. To remain as a tribal entity and develop their resources as a tribal corporation
2. To create an arrangement whereby the members of the tribes may elect to remain on the reservation lands as resident members of the tribes or to leave and be allotted their pro rata share of tribal assets
3. To break up tribal organization and distribute all assets to the members.

In studying these alternatives, the SRI had to consider what resources the tribe possessed, determine economic development opportunities, and assess tribal members' education and training needs.[49]

In February 1961, the business council held a two-day meeting in Nespelem to discuss the findings of the Stanford Research Institute and to poll local tribal members on the options presented. Tribal members split almost evenly, but the sale and distribution of assets won by a narrow margin: 126 members voted for sale and distribution, 123 voted to retain the reservation and develop it, and 118 voted to retain the land and continue the existing system of per capita payments from current income. While this voter turnout may seem small, 367 tribal members represented a majority of eligible voting members residing on the reservation at that time.[50]

When asked if they wanted to distribute proceeds of the sale to the membership or to hold it in trust, the overwhelming majority voted for distribution. The questionnaire did not ask tribal members for a yes or no answer regarding whether they wanted to terminate, only how they wished to achieve termination. That omission would surface repeatedly throughout the Colville termination discussions. The membership never had an opportunity to vote against termination.[51]

A few months later, the tribal council mailed a more detailed poll to all eligible voting members of the tribe, including those who did not live on the reservation. In May of 1961 approximately two thousand questionnaires went out to the membership, and by mid-June roughly two-thirds had been returned and tabulated. The results of the poll, which asked members to choose among the three proposed forms of termination, indicated strong support for termination, but members remained sharply divided on whether to liquidate the assets and divide the money or to start an economic development program and a tribal corporation to manage the resources. The first option represented an immediate per capita payment upon liquidation. The second option allowed for economic development and gradual withdrawal of federal support.[52]

In July 1961, the deadline imposed by P.L. 772, the tribal council submitted a plan for termination. The 1961 plan called for closing the tribal rolls at midnight on the day Congress approved the legislation, holding a referendum as soon as possible after legislative approval to determine whether tribal members wanted to withdraw and/or remain, and gradual withdrawal of federal supervision. The council requested a period of fifteen to twenty years for withdrawal because they believed it would take at least that long for tribal business entities to become well established. The bill was introduced to Congress that year but was tabled until 1962. This first bill inaugurated a decade of similar bills that the Colville Business Council would send to Congress.[53]

Turmoil and infighting among tribal members plagued the reservation between 1961 and 1969. The membership struggled to answer major questions, such as whether full bloods and mixed-bloods had an equal say in matters of tribal government. What about people who lived off the reservation? Eighty percent of off-reservation Colvilles supported termination. Did they have the right to decide for those who lived on the reservation? Members who lived on the reservation had much more at stake in the termination battle. They depended on the government for their health and dental services. As landholders on reservation trust lands, their homes and acreage existed free of county property taxation. Tribal members counted on the BIA to manage the reservation's resources and to protect them from fraud, because that is what the government told Indians to expect. Colville members who lived off the reservation received health services through the county or city where they lived, or had private insurance to pay for them. One termination foe put it this way when considering the tribal laws that allowed off-reservation tribal members to vote on termination:

> We are placing the Indians who live on the reservation at the mercy
> of those who have seen fit to live off the reservation. . . . We are told

from a legal standpoint it is within the authority of the Government
to provide that a reservation shall be governed by residents . . . while
out-of-reservation members may be entitled to such tribal income as
may be set aside for distribution. Our out-of-reservation cousins, more
affluent in metropolitan centers, will always be disturbing factors in
being unmindful of local anxieties and needs.[54]

At the national level, even as planning for Colville termination
commenced, termination as policy began to fall out of favor with Congress. Problems related to Klamath and Menominee termination, both
enacted in 1961, had become evident. Congressional enthusiasm for the
idea of termination really began in the 1940s, in the postwar years,
when homogeneity ruled the day and Indians were both pitied and
feared for their old-fashioned "communal-style" living. Reservations
seemed to be closed societies where common money was distributed
equally to members, a lifestyle that represented something awfully
close to communism or socialism. It took several years for the idea of
termination to gain traction, but Congress finally codified the policy
in 1953.

By the time the Colville Business Council rallied to draft termination bills in the 1960s, however, the nation was in the throes of the Civil
Rights movement and legislators were seeking fair treatment for minorities, at least in theory. This new perspective on race relations meant that
Congress felt less empowered to impose decisions upon tribes, especially
after the problems related to Klamath and Menominee termination
became evident.

Meanwhile, the Colvilles remained well informed of the national
scene throughout the 1950s and 1960s, and they had a strong understanding of how termination affected the Menominee and the Klamath.
While the Menominee and the Klamath terminations in 1961 may seem
too near the Colville timeframe to have offered lessons, the Colvilles witnessed the damages incurred by both tribes in real time. Members of
the council and the tribal attorney had been reading testimony from termination hearings since 1954. They acted as informed individuals.[55] The
impetus for termination originated with a great desire for return of the
North Half. Once that was accomplished, however, why did the Colvilles
continue to pursue termination, especially in the face of evidence of its
harmful results?

For the Colvilles, a greatly factionalized tribe, there is no simple answer. The Colvilles isolated themselves from national Indian movements and politics. They fought with cousins in other Columbia Plateau tribes, such as the Yakama and the Coeur d'Alene, who worried that the loss of federal recognition for the Colvilles would affect their own tribal rolls—and it would have. The Coeur d'Alene Tribe enrolled tribal members based on total Indian blood quantum, not just Coeur d'Alene blood. Consequently, some tribal members were enrolled because of heritage from the Coeur d'Alene Tribe as well as other tribal groups. If the Colvilles terminated successfully, anyone enrolled at Coeur d'Alene who counted Colville blood toward the one-quarter minimum blood quantum for tribal enrollment could have been removed from the tribal rolls if their remaining tribal affiliation did not meet enrollment requirements. The Yakama Tribe's main concern related to shared land and fractionated heirship. Some enrolled Yakama tribal members held fractions of allotted lands on the Colville Reservation, and some Colvilles held similar fractions on the Yakama Reservation. How would Yakama tribal members be compensated for their land holdings on the Colville Reservation if termination proceeded, and what would happen to Colville shares of Yakama land? Both tribes also remained concerned about lost reciprocal hunting and fishing rights if the Colvilles terminated. The Coeur d'Alene Tribe and the Yakama Tribe advanced these concerns at nearly every Colville termination hearing.

Not only did the Colvilles battle outsiders, they fought among themselves. What began as a simple hope, restoration of the North Half, created unprecedented tribal turmoil from which the tribe still has not fully recovered. The business council and the CIA led the termination drive, but the Colville Commercial Club also remained a voice for termination throughout the 1950s and 1960s. In 1963 another pro-termination faction emerged: the Colville Liquidation Promoters (CLP), led by Ruby Babcock and Ira Lum of Omak. While the CIA rejected tribal government as a pawn of the BIA, the CLP actively ran for open council positions under the tagline "Members of Colville Confederated Tribes Promoting Individual Independence." The Colville Liquidation Promoters favored a one-step withdrawal process and wanted it to be completed as soon as possible.

CLP members began their council campaigns in 1963 and by 1965 had won a majority of seats on the tribal council. The CLP ran effective—and nasty—campaigns, and members of the CLP held their majority on the tribal council until 1971. The CLP's platform of rapid termination and distribution of per capita payments from all tribal monies and assets proved tempting for many Colvilles, both on and off the reservation. Money obviously played a big role in continued consideration of termination, and it is important to remember that many tribal members on the reservation had incomes well below the national average. In 1952 the average family income in the United States was $3,900. On the Colville Reservation, it was $1,712.[56] In addition, tribal members had been waiting for payment from the original sale of the North Half and for payments related to construction of and power generation from the Grand Coulee Dam for decades by this point.[57]

Pro-terminationists were not the only leaders in the community, however. Two formal groups opposed termination. The Petitioners Party, led by Paschal Sherman and T. B. Charley,[58] rejected termination and liquidation. Initially the Petitioners Party asked the federal government, if termination indeed proved inevitable, to preserve the reservation under conservation principles similar to those applied to national parks and national forests, as part of the nation's heritage.[59] Subsequently this group opposed termination in any form. The Committee on Indian Rights also fought termination. They emerged near the end of the termination debate, and their platform remained absolute opposition to the policy. They would eventually win a majority of seats on the tribal council in 1971.

The less-formalized resistance to termination may be attributable to the fact that anti-terminationists did not have to write a bill to ensure that the Colville Tribes would remain. They just had to keep voting against bills to terminate the tribe. This kind of resistance can also be viewed as disagreement voiced by nonparticipation, similar to the IRA vote. Resistance by this method—a refusal to participate—is the reason pro-terminationists remained so tied to the language in termination bills calling for passage of termination by a majority of members voting, rather than by a majority of members eligible to vote. Authors of Colville termination bills felt that the majority-of-voters clause gave unfair advantage to people who simply refused to participate, because the authors knew what nonparticipation meant. Based on negative experiences with both IRA and termination actions decided by a majority of members voting, the BIA and other elected officials remained steadfast in their opposition to this language in the Colville termination bills.

Just as the Colville leadership began aggressively pursuing termination, Congress and the president had begun a quiet retreat from the policy.[60] The policy had led to a once-successful tribe's downward spiral when the Menominees had to sell land and tribal enterprises in order to pay their local property taxes. It also left the Klamath, a formerly land- and timber-rich community, destitute and without a homeland. Many members of both communities relied on state assistance after termination, where few had before, creating a new economic burden on the states the breadth of which the federal government had not anticipated. The magnitude of these tribes' losses still did not dissuade pro-termination Colvilles. The leadership remained confident that their members would not meet similar fates. Bureau of Indian Affairs commissioner Philleo Nash agreed: "It is not part of the thinking of this department that Colvilles, either on or off the reservation, are likely to dissipate cash assets if placed in their hands."[61]

The 1963 hearings, and each of the hearings afterward, illustrated the divisions within the tribe and brought private disagreements into the national dialogue. As Congress turned away from termination, the Colvilles would be the most notable group still involved in the process. Their debate and internal discord received local and national media attention, and organized Indian groups spoke at length about the damage the Colvilles might do with their initiatives. As leaders on the national scene such as Helen Peterson and Vine Deloria Jr., both executive directors of the National Congress of American Indians during the 1960s, spoke out against termination, local termination opponents also emerged as strong tribal leaders.

Council member Lucy Covington remains the most recognized name in the fight against Colville termination. She garnered the respect of Congress members with her eloquence and demeanor during this contentious time. Covington won election to a tribal council comprised mainly of pro-terminationist Colville Liquidation Promoters and held her seat through the end of the termination debate and beyond. She became the first woman elected as chair of the tribal council. A descendant of Chief Moses, the leader who moved his band to the Colville Reservation and joined the confederation, and a mixed-blood tribal member, Covington proved formidable in her fight against termination.[62] The Affiliated Tribes of Northwest Indians recognized Covington's contribution in 1969 and praised her commitment to the cause while pro-terminationists controlled the tribal media and tribal council. "She had to work the roads, the streets, and the fields, searching out and talking to tribal members" in order to build a majority among local voters in opposition to termination so that "they would not be outnumbered by the expected avalanche of terminationist votes from the absentees."[63]

While Lucy Covington may be the most recognized name from this period, Colville leaders Frank George and Paschal Sherman worked at both the national level and the local level to prevent termination. And, although the leaders of pro-termination factions are not remembered as often, the determination of Marcel Arcasa of the CIA and Ruby Babcock of the CLP cannot be underestimated. These two groups and their membership kept this debate going for nearly a decade after many national leaders and government officials would have let Colville termination drop. To mention all of the important participants on both sides of the debate would be unwieldy, but it is important to note that the leaders referenced here represent only a sampling of activists on both sides of this debate. The unnamed participants were just as integral to the process.

Individual testimonies at the various congressional hearings throw tribal members' positions into touching relief. The vocal pleas for or against termination illustrated how broadly tribal members interpreted what the policy would mean for them. Some viewed termination as freedom—a chance to manage their own land holdings and finances and to live without government oversight. Others viewed the policy as yet another broken promise in a long line of broken promises emanating from Washington, DC. Some reservation tribal members feared loss of land and loss of identity. Tribal members who lived far from the reservation embraced the opportunity to receive a monetary boost for the sale of lands they never planned to inhabit.

Termination presented complexities for everyone. Members of Congress pursued approval for the policy, then changed their minds when they realized how damaging application of the policy turned out to be. Indian organizations, including the National Congress of American Indians and the Affiliated Tribes of Northwest Indians, opposed the policy wholesale but felt torn when their Colville members earnestly requested support for their termination hopes. Colville tribal members experienced the most confusion, as leaders on both sides of the debate made persuasive cases for approving or rejecting the policy. Restoration of the

North Half in 1956 seemed to go largely unnoticed because of the preoccupation over termination. What should have been a time of celebration was instead a time of discord and confusion. Out of that confusion grew a power struggle for control of the reservation. Would the BIA remain patriarchal overseers of the tribal government through manipulation of the council, or would the independent leaders of the reservation, as embodied by the CIA, win back control for the people and set tribal members free to govern their own affairs? This question and the fight it initiated sustained the Colville termination battle and sometimes still resonate today.

HILLS OVERLOOKING COULEE CORRIDOR (HIGHWAY 155) BETWEEN COLVILLE AGENCY AND GRAND COULEE DAM

CHAPTER 2

"It is like giving your eagle feather away."

HE Colvilles had initiated termination when they accepted restoration of the North Half in 1956, but many tribal members and
the business council hoped that congressional opinion would
turn sharply enough against termination that they would not ultimately
have to create a termination plan. But as the 1961 deadline mandated
by restoration neared, the Bureau of Indian Affairs made it clear to the
council that they were still responsible for drafting a plan. As the council
considered how to prioritize community needs, they retained the Stanford Research Institute (SRI) to analyze options for Colville termination
and began serious work on the first Colville termination plan. The SRI's
assessments would inform the council's first termination bill in 1961, as
well as each subsequent termination bill throughout the 1960s.

The council and the BIA were aware of the Stanford Research Institute
because of its work on Klamath termination. Taking its parameters from
the business council, the SRI outlined the options for Colville termination: tribal members could choose to remain a tribal entity and develop
their resources as a tribal corporation; some tribal members could withdraw and accept payment for their share of the tribal resources while
others remained on a reduced reservation; or the Colvilles could choose
complete liquidation and distribution of assets in one immediate cash
payment.

The council had charged the SRI with designing a plan for termination, but the option to remain a tribal entity and develop resources as

a tribal corporation represented the nearest option to not terminating at all. In this scenario, the tribe would be without federal supervision but would retain its property and financial assets and could continue to develop the assets as a corporation. The tribal constitution would no longer be in effect, so the tribe would not have control over law and order or health care, but the corporation would create investment and development strategies that could reflect tribal aims. With termination, the Colville Tribe would no longer exist; rather than being members of the Colville Tribes, individuals would become shareholders in the corporation.

The second termination option offered equal representation to those who wanted to withdraw from the Colville community and those who wanted to remain affiliated with it. Members could vote to withdraw from the Colville entity and take an individual share of the assets or could choose to remain on the Colville land base and be entitled to services and individual shares of revenues that might be generated from a possible Colville corporation. This option was designed to serve the needs of both pro- and anti-terminationists, but also proved to be the most problematic. If too many tribal members chose to withdraw upon termination, too much of the tribal land base and resources would have to be sold to accommodate a buyout of the withdrawing members. Consequently, the remaining members could be left with a dramatically reduced land base that would limit economic development opportunities in forest industries, recreation industries, and mining.

The final option provided by the SRI seemed the most straightforward. Tribal members could choose complete liquidation of tribal assets followed by a per capita payment to each tribal member. Tribal members who favored this option imagined a great financial windfall, but as the 1960s progressed, asset valuation proved difficult. The Colville Tribes had great timberlands and water and mineral rights, as well as a negotiated share of revenue from the Grand Coulee Dam. While the Bonneville Power Administration had yet to make good on payments related to Grand Coulee, that revenue would have to be included in the liquidation formula. In addition, human resources would also have to be included in any valuation. As enrolled tribal members, individuals could use the Bureau of Indian Affairs health services not just on the Colville Reservation but on any reservation. Tribal members had access to funds for education and job training, as well as preferred hiring in tribal industries on the Colville Reservation and often on other reservations too. The value of hunting and fishing rights on the Colville Reservation, both for Colville tribal members and members of other tribes, would also need to be included in the liquidation assessment. Federal officials found it difficult to assign a dollar value to these latter benefits because they represented more of a community right than a quantifiable asset. Moreover, the timber and mineral resources proved difficult to quantify because the market value frequently fluctuated.

In February 1961 the tribal council, under the direction of chairman Harvey Moses, held the first of several tribal meetings at the Nespelem agency to introduce details of the SRI report to the Colville community and to discuss the options in greater detail. The council members sat at a long table at the front of the room and faced rows of tribal members seated on wooden and metal chairs stretching from wall to wall. The council viewed these meetings as integral to the development of a Colville plan and encouraged tribal members to participate and share their perspectives on termination; the tribal members who could translated the discussions into the Colville dialects for the elders who largely still spoke Salish and Sahaptian dialects.

The meeting began with questions from the floor about why tribal members had not been consulted prior to the creation of P.L. 772. Some tribal members believed that they should have been involved in this first step toward termination, especially since not all of the tribal members wanted to terminate. Mrs. Leo Crossland of Monse, Washington, near the northern border of the reservation, suggested that the people deserved to get another council because the sitting council had acted without consulting tribal members. She also observed, "Liquidating today doesn't mean payment tomorrow."[1]

One tribal member wondered why, if the SRI report had found potential for development, no development had begun before now. The SRI report had indicated that it would be possible for a tribal corporation to operate after termination if sufficient timber and land resources remained. The report did not offer specific methods for economic development; it noted only that development could be accomplished. This criticism about lack of economic development by the tribe would pervade future discussions. In this meeting, tribal members suggested that a slow-to-act tribal council pandered to a controlling BIA that did not want to invest funds in the reservation. Others thought that the tribal members were too indifferent to act. A leader of the Colville Indian Association (CIA), Marcel Arcasa of Nespelem, told the group that education and training, as well as development, should be made available to tribal members in order to make the reservation function better as a whole. If tribal members had these advantages, then termination would not be necessary or desirable. Lucy Swan, a member of the Lakes band and resident of Inchelium and also a leader in the CIA, favored termination, but prior to approving it, she wanted the council to demand full payment from the government for other transactions:

> The government needs to make restitution for several instances where Indians have not been given full payment for value received. [We] want payment for the Colville Valley and for loss of salmon fishing at Kettle Falls. We want royalties from the Grand Coulee Dam. We want to get rid of the Bureau of Indian Affairs and the council.[2]

Alyce Hallenius of Omak reminded fellow tribal members that in the Indian concept, land represented more than real estate. "In the Indian sense land stands for existence, identity, a place of belonging. This is the significance the Indians are asked to destroy, and understandably they hesitate. Indian rights and liberties cannot be sold." At the end of the meeting, the council distributed ballots for the tribal members to vote for their preference of the three options presented by the SRI report. It is obvious from the discussions that few tribal members fully comprehended what termination and liquidation would mean. Many felt that they could be without supervision, but not without services or privileges. Few understood that to accept any aspect of termination meant acceptance of the whole idea.

The ballots provided at the meetings did not ask whether or not tribal members wanted to terminate, but whether they favored liquidation, development, or a continuation of the current per capita dispersal system. The comments submitted in the remarks section of the ballots illustrated the level of division and misunderstanding that this question created. Twenty-five percent of the tribal members voting shared their opinions on termination or their reasons for voting the way they did. Many Colvilles favored development. Others feared a lack of preparation among tribal members for the eventual effects of termination. "Indian is not ready for termination," one person wrote, adding, "A lot of old people do not understand what liquidation or termination is!" Another reminded the ballot counters, "In union there is strength."[3] One supporter of termination wrote, "I would like to have what I have coming and live like everyone else in the world," while another wrote, "Time we become real Americans and joined the rest of the country." Some tribal members wanted to retain the reservation, but not the BIA or the tribal council; "I think there should be an abolishment of this Indian Bureau. I don't see why Indians should be dominated all their lives."[4]

Liquidation won by a narrow margin. In this first informal reservation survey, tribal members indicated that they desired complete liquidation of tribal resources and per capita payments to each tribal member. The majority did not want the proceeds of a tribal liquidation held in trust by a tribal corporation or reinvested by that corporation.[5] The director of the Portland area BIA office considered the results "interesting but inconclusive and perhaps not really indicative of the opinions of the members because of the possibility for misunderstanding some of the questions."[6] The director had not been to the Colville Reservation to participate in the termination discussions, and his assessment upon reading the meeting minutes represents the commonly held BIA position that Indian opinions must be verified by federal officials before they could be trusted.

The tribal council created committees of tribal members in each district to poll their neighbors on termination. Throughout the spring, the council and the committees worked to create a questionnaire that would generate a more accurate interpretation of tribal members' opinions. In May the council mailed out roughly two thousand opinion polls to all adult members of the tribe, including those who resided off the reservation. By mid-June, two-thirds of the adult membership had responded to the questionnaire, and the council created Planning Report Number 3 to incorporate the results. Sixty-five percent of the respondents lived off the reservation, and 72 percent were under fifty years of age, numbers that aligned closely with the demographic distribution of the Colville membership.[7] Distinct yes or no votes on termination did not emerge from the opinion poll because the council only asked how tribal members wanted to implement termination, not whether they wanted to terminate. The council concluded, however, that roughly one third of the respondents favored termination.[8] In ensuing years, pro-terminationists would estimate that 50 to 75 percent of tribal members favored termination. Those numbers would start to fall again only as the 1960s drew to a close.

While the results of the various surveys did not provide total clarity, the council used them as foundation for the draft termination legislation. The draft submitted to the secretary of the Interior on July 12, 1961, would be introduced to Congress as House Resolution 8469 in August. The tribal council knew that it was not a perfect bill but felt pressed by the deadline inherent in P.L. 772.[9]

The BIA and the Department of the Interior had been following the public reservation discussions about termination and had also received many letters in favor of and in opposition to termination. Both departments shared this information with the Subcommittee on Indian Affairs, which was part of the Committee on Interior and Insular Affairs in the House of Representatives and the Senate from 1947 to 1977. The subcommittee took no action on the bill in 1961 because it came in near the end of that congressional session, but when it reconvened about the bill in May 1962, committee members had strong background information for their discussion of the proposed termination. In concert with H.R. 8469, the committee also reviewed H.R. 6801, a bill submitted by Thor Tollefson at the behest of the Colville Indian Association, which had drafted the bill. Tollefson's district was in Seattle, not near the reservation, and his bill spoke more to the desires of off-reservation Indians who favored quick termination and the liquidation of tribal assets.

H.R. 6801 proved unworkable in myriad ways, but the committee's primary concern lay in the proposed method for timber disposition. The Colville Reservation contained roughly four billion board feet of timber. It takes about three thousand board feet to build a one-thousand-square-foot house; Colville timber could have built roughly 1.3 million homes. The CIA bill suggested total liquidation of timber assets, not allowing for sustained yield, and a cash payout of the money from the sale. The CIA believed that no timber buyer would support a sustained yield purchase, since timber prices fluctuate, and they also argued that a sustained yield clause would impair the Colvilles' ability to sell the resource. The CIA did not appear to consider, however, that timber sales supported a large portion of the tribal budget. If timber liquidation and distribution of funds to individuals occurred, then tribal programs would suffer severely. Because H.R. 6801 proposed to allow those unwilling to terminate to remain and to develop economic opportunities on the remaining land, complete disposition of the timber would not be possible.

Furthermore, subcommittee members shied away from the phrase "fair market value" used in the bill, because they had begun to experience repercussions from the Klamath termination legislation containing that same language. Fair market value fluctuated with the market, sometimes significantly, which made a concrete dollar amount difficult to know. The Klamaths had litigated before the Indian Claims Commission because of the discrepancy in the compensation they received to terminate. The estimate for payout provided during the Klamath debate differed considerably from the actual payment because the timber markets had softened by the time Congress enacted the bill. The Klamaths had negotiated a price millions of dollars higher than their final payout. When the timber marketed softened after the Klamaths had approved termination, Congress passed a bill to modify the final termination payment, and, with that new dollar amount recorded, passed a bill finalizing termination. The difference in the negotiated amount and the final amount represented roughly $10,000 to $15,000 per tribal member. It also illustrated how much Indian communities were at the mercy of Congress and the BIA. An agreement made in good faith was simply set aside when economics softened the deal. As a result, government officials from the departments of Agriculture and the Interior feared using the same language in the Colville case.[10]

Beyond these considerations, the CIA bill contained a tangle of conflicting thirty-day, sixty-day, and six-month requirements for closure of the rolls, which made the framework for being recognized, defined, and counted as a Colville unworkable. The government's responsibility at each level of termination or remaining also proved hazy. Would the BIA initiate the process and had it committed to managing the process? And would the Department of the Interior be responsible for natural resource evaluation figures? The answers were unclear, and as a result, the subcommittee did not support the bill.[11]

The CIA was not dissuaded by this defeat. They vigorously embraced the idea of termination and actively endeavored to convert the concept into reality. Over the next several years, they would become more conversant with structuring legislation and vocal in their support of termination, and they would witness the success of their pro-termination cohort in winning a majority of seats on the tribal business council.[12]

No tribal members sent written testimony and none appeared in person at the 1962 hearings before the subcommittee. In later years, Colville tribal members and the tribal council would actively engage with the subcommittee at hearings and via correspondence, but in 1962 only government officials from the departments of Interior, Agriculture, and Budget testified or sent written comments in regard to the readiness of the Colvilles for termination. Philleo Nash, commissioner of Indian Affairs,[13] highlighted the distinction between the needs of reservation residents and off-reservation tribal members, not giving either legitimacy over the other but noting that the proposed disposition in H.R. 6801 would more severely affect the 25 percent of tribal members who lived on the reservation. The timber sale would provide a nice dividend for off-reservation members, but it would mean a reduction in services such as health care, education, and assistance to those members who still lived in the area.[14]

Chairman of the subcommittee Wayne Aspinall queried whether the off-reservation group would support a solution similar to the Klamath termination, and wondered if the Colvilles would be ready to vote on termination in the near future. Nash cited the Stanford Research Institute's findings that 55 percent of tribal members opposed termination, and declared that no simple plan had been outlined so far. Even he found the Stanford report too complex and too long to be clearly understood. The tribal council had requested further study, and Nash suggested to the subcommittee that they learn from the collective pre-termination processes of the Klamath and Menominee tribes to prepare the Colvilles more thoroughly before asking them to vote.[15]

While the subcommittee engaged with federal departments about termination, candidates for the Colville Tribal Council launched their election campaigns. Frank Moore of the CIA created a protest ballot to be submitted in place of approved election ballots and organized tribal members to use them. Thirty percent of tribal members voting by absentee ballot in the 1962 tribal council elections submitted protest ballots. This ballot actively opposed federal government control over tribal assets. It read:

I Will Not Vote in the 1962 Colville Election for Councilmen for the following reason which I choose to check:

1. The tribal members do not have any voice in tribal policies or termination.
2. Council is controlled by cliques, personal views and gains, Indian Bureau policies and interference by the National Congress of American Indians and like groups.
3. No control over spending and waste of tribal money.
4. The only amendments to the tribal constitution approved by election which are allowed to become effective are those which increase council power. Those election results which would decrease council power are nullified by the Indian Bureau.
5. None of the 75 percent off-reservation members allowed to serve on council.
6. Last year's election results which turned down negotiating and legislating powers for the council by a vote of 3 to 1 [were] not permitted by Department of Interior to restrict council actions.
7. Termination issues have not been put squarely to the people. The group leader system is a farce.
8. Colville tribal members are competent and have enough statistical information for an immediate termination decision.
9. Development programs planned by council and Indian Bureau will tie up property and judgment money against people's expressed wishes.
10. People and property held in communal status by use of council system.
11. I desire an election which will give all enrolled tribal members the right to express an opinion on continued existence of tribal entity.

I am signing and mailing only one of these sheets
(signed) *Enrolled Member, Colville Confederated Tribes*
I desire an immediate free election on termination method.[16]

The protest ballot provides a riveting snapshot of the protestors. Voters rejected the tribal council structure and practices, and demanded more individual input. This desire for stronger self-government and greater community control reflected their desire for termination. High levels of engagement with the protest ballot indicated support for the CIA position. Moore sent a copy of the ballot along with a letter to the Subcommittee on Indian Affairs and asserted, "Current policies of the executive branch of the U.S. Government do not appear to consider the rights of the individual Indian, but do intend to enforce a wholesale communal status wherever possible."[17] Once pro-terminationists gained control of the tribal council, they rectified some complaints from the ballot. They severed ties with the National Congress of American Indians and other Indian associations, and they put the question of termination directly to the people through numerous meetings and nonbinding votes about whether to terminate.

Termination became a highly complex issue for tribal members. The discussions extracted very personal observations about financial issues and social values, and the dialogue also resulted in frank assessments of what the BIA had done for the Colvilles and where it had failed them. Most importantly, the debate and testimony offered by the Colvilles provide a human perspective on a federal policy. The Colvilles spoke with eloquence and emotion, and with credulity. Prior to the first open hearings on Colville termination in Spokane, Washington, in 1963, tribal members expressed their opinions through letters to department officials, and to President John F. Kennedy and Attorney General Robert Kennedy. They likely addressed the Kennedy brothers because they believed the two sought to protect Indian rights. While campaigning for the presidency, Kennedy had promised Indians that his administration would reject Republican policies on Indian affairs and that he would not change treaty or contractual agreements without consent from the tribes affected.[18] After a meeting with Frank George, chairman of the American Indian Section of the Nationalities Division of the Democratic National Committee, during his presidential campaign, Senator Kennedy assured members of the Nationalities Division, "The Democratic Party recognizes the unique legal and moral responsibility of the Federal Government for Indians in restitution for the injustice that has sometimes been done to them. . . . Our platform pledges prompt adoption of a program to assist Indian tribes in the full development of their human and natural resources and to advance the health, education, and economic well-being of Indian citizens while preserving their cultural heritage." Tribal members credited Kennedy for his position but also felt no compunction about reminding Kennedy of his duty to them.

In one letter, Marian Bourgeau of Inchelium explained to President Kennedy that the Indian had always been self-supporting and did not benefit greatly from the BIA. Nevertheless she wanted to retain the reservation and BIA supervision:

Mr. Udall on T.V. this morning has said that the Indian should be ready to help themselves. Well, what do you suppose we've been doing all these years? We've been taking care of ourselves. If we had waited for the Government or the Bureau of Indian Affairs to help us, we would have starved many years ago. It sounds rather ignorant the way Mr. Udall had put it. . . . Mr. Kennedy maybe you can help us keep our land and our reservation.[19]

The Department of the Interior recognized that many Colvilles had had extensive dealings with their white neighbors and that many had achieved at least an average level of education—when compared to other Indians. The fact sheet on the Colvilles in 1962 assessed the tribes in this way:

94 percent of the tribal families were economically independent by minimum standards. . . . Approximately 80 percent of the tribal members have finished the eighth grade. . . . About 75 percent of the adults reside off the reservation. Of these less than 1 percent, all elderly, reportedly do not speak English. The educational levels achieved by the members of the Tribes compare favorably with or slightly excel the levels achieved by American Indians in general. The Colville Indians have retained many of their Indian ceremonial customs and at the same time have adopted cultural customs of their white neighbors. As a group they are intelligent, thrifty, and industrious in developing homes, farms, and ranges. The Confederated Tribes are generally able to manage their own affairs.[20]

In light of these statistics, the Interior Department classified the Colvilles as competent, which allowed Congress to proceed with the termination legislation, and the tribal council created H.R. 8469. Several more tribal council bills would follow throughout the 1960s, but all of them found some part of their template in this bill. House Resolution 8469 did not set a termination date but outlined a plan to achieve that goal. It offered a two-phase approach, which began with the closure of the tribal rolls on the day Congress enacted the proposed legislation, initiating an important first step in determining who could be counted as Colville. Questions of enrollment can often be sensitive issues, and assertions of membership and fights over blood quantum would emerge with a vengeance during the years the Colvilles debated termination. Colville blood quantum is measured according to ancestry in one or more of the twelve bands that reside on the Colville Reservation. Contemporary enrollment regulations require one-quarter or more Colville blood from any of the twelve bands. This requirement can be met through affiliation in a single band, or ancestry from more than one band may be combined to meet this requirement. The ancestry can be traced from matrilineal, patrilineal, or both bloodlines. During the termination era, tribal members could be counted with as little as one-eighth Colville blood from any of the twelve bands because enrollment allowed membership based on blood quantum as well as tracing of family names to the roll at the time the tribe approved the tribal constitution. Enrollment determined who had a voice in these debates, but it also governed who would get a payment from the liquidation of assets. The closing of the rolls also meant that, even if official termination legislation did not proceed, the Colville Tribe would eventually cease to exist.

Discussions of blood quantum would consistently appear in Colville termination discussions. Tribal members were right to pay such close attention to the issue. The Ute tribes of Utah used blood quantum to differentiate among tribal members, and, when faced with creating termination legislation, the Uncompahgre and Whiteriver full-blood members set themselves apart from the mixed-blood Uintah members. While the full-bloods retained their land and their tribal designation, they sacrificed the mixed-bloods to termination.[21]

H.R. 8469 provided that after the BIA declared and published the final rolls, the Colvilles would have their property bequeathed to them, so that even when the reservation ceased to exist, they would still remain on their land. This section also removed tax liabilities normally associated with inheritance and property ownership, since Indians are exempt from property taxes when their land is held in tribal trust. The next step in the process required the secretary of the Interior to update all the ownership records for reservation lands and to complete a mineral survey of the reservation. While Nash characterized this portion of his responsibility as "not an impossible task,"[22] the mineral valuation would prove to be less simple than he imagined. Producing a dollar value for minerals remained a vexing process throughout the Colville termination debate.

Land valuations also had to be calculated to produce a reasonable offer for the disposition. This valuation had to take into consideration allotments, as well as timberland, agricultural areas, and grazing lands. The Interior Department needed to conduct a thorough review of the land and grazing leases, which the Stanford Research Institute had already begun. The SRI's initial findings indicated that current lessees paid far less than market value, sometimes as much as 27 percent less, for agricultural and grazing leases. Lease agreements stayed on par with the market rate when the BIA negotiated leases on behalf of tribal members.[23]

The Colvilles provided for protection of their water rights in the post-termination era by requiring the state of Washington to allow them preferential use of surface and subsurface water on and around the reservation. The council was much less proactive in protecting hunting and fishing rights. Given the amount of concern tribal members had voiced about this specific issue, the forfeiture of the hunting and fishing rights upon sale of the reservation constituted a surprising concession. Various interpretations of the value of hunting and fishing rights, and whether tribal members should retain them, would also appear in subsequent bills.[24]

A large part of the subcommittee discussion relating to H.R. 8469 concerned the findings of the Stanford Research Institute survey regarding which approach to termination would be most effective. The committee considered the SRI report in the format received by the tribe and reviewed the options for termination: to continue the reservation resources as a group endeavor without any further development, but maintaining leases and other activities presently constituted; to undertake a program to develop the reservation resources on their own or with help; or to liquidate all the assets and distribute the pro rate shares to all members.[25]

All future Colville termination bills referred to these options, and each bill presented a variation of combinations of the SRI's proposed solutions. At the 1962 hearing, the Interior Department argued against liquidation and distribution because that option did not represent each tribal member's needs. Tribal members who had not lived off the reservation and who still depended on hunting, fishing, and root and berry harvesting for sustenance would lose access to their resources if termination occurred. Udall and Nash favored the development and management of tribal resources, which translated to a more gradual withdrawal of federal supervision. The Interior also favored a slower approach to termination so that the department and the Colvilles would have more time to discuss issues of jurisdiction with the state of Washington and with Ferry and Okanogan counties. Once the land came under county and state landholdings and jurisdiction, the counties and the state would absorb the responsibilities related to law and order and the health and welfare of tribal members. Commissioner Nash had observed early indications of the damage that rapid termination had caused Klamath and Menominee tribal members—loss of land and homes due to unpaid property taxes in the Menominee case, and loss of termination payments due to inexperienced money management in the Klamath case—since termination the previous year and did not wish to replicate the experience for the Colvilles.

Nash also reported that the Colville Tribal Council had visited the Klamaths to see the result of their termination process. That visit reinforced the council's resolve to avoid the complete liquidation of assets favored by the CIA, but did not dissuade council members from moving forward with termination. The two-step process endorsed by both the Interior and the council, then, called for the closure of the rolls and the identification of Colville tribal members, along with discussions about the valuations and dollar amounts. The second step, actual removal of federal supervision, would not be given as a specific date within the legislation but would instead be a time frame, a mutual goal for assessing the moment when the Colvilles had effective systems in place and could manage without BIA oversight. Nash concluded his testimony, "We are not wedded to a perpetual Federal trust, we are wedded to the idea of management for the national and the individual good."[26]

At the conclusion of Nash's testimony, Congressman James Haley of Florida, a subcommittee chair, joined Nash in expressing his own desire to do right by the Indian: "It has always been the desire of the chairman to try and protect the Indians as much as he possibly can. As a matter of fact, someone said not long ago if I had a soft spot in my heart, which they doubted, it was for the Indians."[27] Nash and Haley supported greater Indian control over tribal lands, development, and human resources. They did not seek to impose termination on tribes who rejected it, but they did anticipate a lessening of government oversight related to Indian affairs. The most vocal supporter of termination of federal responsibility, Senator Arthur Watkins of Utah, who desired a complete severance of federal responsibility to Indian communities and peoples, perceived reduced oversight as indistinct from removal of federal supervision. He maintained that if tribes could progress with reduced federal management, the time had come for the BIA to release these tribes from government control.

Watkins wrote the original termination legislation in 1953, and a few years later he wrote an essay to more clearly define his position. In the essay, he characterized Congress as endeavoring "in the nineteenth and early twentieth century to free the Indian. A full study of congressional actions will bear this out. Freedom for the Indian was the goal then; it is the goal now."[28] Watkins barely concealed his disdain for the Indian Reorganization Act, a policy designed to return cultural and political oversight of tribal affairs to tribal governments, and summarized the IRA as causing the Indians to be delayed in their achievement of "full freedom." He also lamented the special interest groups who were appealing to Congress members to reject termination legislation. The motivation of those interlopers, he charged, was a desire to keep Indians apart from the rest of American society. Watkins also depicted the Indian Claims Commission as a crucial component leading to Indians' freedom "by assuring final settlement of all obligations—real or purported—of the federal government to the Indian tribes and other groups."[29]

Watkins lost his Senate seat in 1959, but the termination initiatives he launched would continue to affect Indian Country for decades. The Menominee and the Klamath did not terminate until 1961, well after Watkins left office, but they owed their termination directly to the policy he designed. His reach also extended to the Colvilles, who tried to follow the termination agreement they had made in exchange for the North Half even as they tried to integrate the lessons of the Menominee and Klamath terminations.

While Colville tribal members had their own reasons for wanting to terminate or wanting to remain, in the beginning the tribal council simply used termination as a tool to regain the lost North Half. In discussions with the government, the council also expressed interest in better job training and educational programs so that tribal members would not be forever dependant on welfare. The tribal council articulated their hope for termination this way in 1955: "Our people are desirous of becoming self-supporting, self-respecting, self-reliant and exclusive of any form of public assistance."[30] Some tribal members simply wanted to be out from under the government's thumb. Others, like Lucy Covington, desired to avoid termination: "Termination is something no Indian should ever dream about. It is like giving your eagle feather away."[31]

By 1962 shadows of termination's failures could be glimpsed, but the damage remained minimal. The Menominee had their own county and corporation and had not yet been forced to begin selling land in order to pay their taxes. The Klamath had gotten their payout, and many had scattered but a few had returned destitute with nowhere to go and no job skills to support them. The Klamaths had received a $43,000 per capita payment for terminating, and the businesses in surrounding towns welcomed Indian trade like never before. Car dealerships, appliance stores, and many other merchants offered special Indian prices, significantly higher that what others paid. One Colville tribal member remembers being in Oregon shortly after the payout and socializing with Klamaths in a local bar. All the Indians at the table carried their per capita money in brown paper grocery bags, and each threw money in as the rounds of drinks and food kept coming. No one kept track of the tab, and it is certain that this group continued to overpay as the night wore on.

The Klamath example provided a strong argument for the two-step withdrawal process that the tribal council and the Interior Department advocated at that time. Both recognized the need for job training and education in simple life skills. Many Colvilles did not have checking accounts or credit accounts, but paid for everything in cash. The Colvilles did not hold on to their money out of ignorance of financial institutions. Because much of the reservation remained sparsely populated, not many towns had banks. It was much easier to hold on to cash and manage household accounts in that fashion than it was to visit a bank during business hours.

The two-step process can also be interpreted as building in one more defense against final termination. Many council members and tribal members did not actually believe that they would have to terminate. Several testified to this during the congressional hearings throughout the 1960s. While the one-step liquidation process could provide a one-time valuation of assets, and a per capita payout from the proceeds appealed to tribal members because of the large dollar amount associated with it—estimates of $30,000 to $80,000 per person circulated throughout the termination years—the payout also rang with a resounding finality. If Congress passed the one-step, single-option liquidation act that the

CIA advocated, then the Colville Confederated Tribes would lose their federal recognition in one fell swoop. The two-step process provided the tribe and tribal members with a planning period of indeterminate length. Tribal members had lived through shifts in federal Indian policy before—perhaps termination opponents hoped that the second phase of termination would last long enough that Congress and the BIA would make another policy change, one that would eliminate termination altogether.

Termination enjoyed a brief but damaging reign as a federal policy. The importance of termination history lies not with the policy or its authors but with the people affected by it. At the 1962 hearing, the Subcommittee on Indian Affairs determined to hold other hearings on or near the Colville Reservation, or in cities where a large population of Colvilles lived. At these hearings, Colville stories resonated with pride in being Indian, with dismay at the thought of losing their homeland, with frustration with the Indian bureau, and with appeals to Congress to help them, to protect them, and to do right by them. Throughout this period, the Subcommittee on Indian Affairs remained placid, though not indifferent, toward the Colvilles' pursuit of termination. Colville tribal members, however, became energized by the debate and vocal in their support for or opposition to termination. That energy would drive the debate for a decade.

CACHE CREEK ROAD, FACING EAST FROM NESPELEM TOWARD KELLER

CHAPTER 3

"Soon buried in a junk pile of Cadillacs."

A
S the Colville Business Council continued to advance termination, the Subcommittee on Indian Affairs decided to hold hearings among the Colvilles to ascertain their opinions on termination. This journey to the reservation would inaugurate an era of unprecedented open dialogue between the Colvilles and the subcommittee, and the three-day hearings resulted in nearly 250 recorded statements. From October 24 to 26, 1963, members of the committee held hearings in Washington State—in Spokane; in Nespelem, the BIA agency seat; and in Seattle. Ninety-seven people either testified or submitted statements at these hearings, all but a handful of them tribal members. Another 146 people submitted written statements—letters of support or opposition—during the two weeks following the hearings while the record remained open.

The testimonies provide a fascinating snapshot of the tribal temper in 1963. Surprisingly few people, roughly a dozen, voiced absolute opposition to termination. Most testifying objected to the tribal council bill, S. 1442, and favored instead H.R. 4918, a bill submitted on behalf of the Colville Indian Association. The CIA's mobilization effort proved extremely effective, as it produced vocal and articulate tribal members who called for an immediate and one-step plan. CIA members unanimously labeled S. 1442 a fraudulent termination bill that represented only the needs of a corrupt business council and a paternalistic Bureau of Indian Affairs. The CIA found its support primarily among the off-reservation members.

The Petitioners Party also opposed S. 1442. Dr. Paschal Sherman led this group, the only organized group against termination at this time, and his testimony offered a unique solution to the termination question. He assumed that some change in the status of the reservation would be inevitable, but he asked the committee to consider converting the reservation into a forest preserve and national park instead of selling it off and dividing it. Citing president John F. Kennedy's desire to protect the nation's natural resources, Sherman envisioned his solution as a win-win situation. More than four hundred tribal members across the reservation joined him in support of this idea. Sherman, also called Quas-quay or Blue-jay, had grown up on the reservation but lived in Washington, DC, for most of his adult life. Sherman was the first tribal member to attain a PhD and he also held an LLB degree, both from Catholic University of America. He served as an officer of the National Congress of American Indians during the 1950s, and after he retired from the Department of Veterans Affairs in 1962, he became actively engaged in Colville termination.

The Colville Liquidation Promoters officially organized in 1963, in response to Colville termination. Founder and president Ruby Babcock asserted in a *Spokesman-Review* interview in April of 1963, "We are not connected with any other Indian group." The CLP formed in order to demand "No strings and no controls, just liquidation of the Colville Indian Reservation." Many CIA members had defected to join the CLP because the CLP intended to get candidates on the ballot for the May elections and seize control of the tribal council in order to advance their single-step liquidation plan. The CLP would only endorse their own candidates, and Babcock pledged to actively campaign for them. As a tribal member, Babcock understood how Indians often expressed opposition through silence. When she announced the CLP's plans, she noted, "We want the Indians to express themselves at the polls and not stay away in silent demonstration."[1] Colville Liquidation Promoters candidates would not win the majority in 1963, but by 1965 they would control the tribal council. Because the CLP wanted an immediate and final termination action that would liquidate and distribute assets, they opposed S. 1442. While they reasserted that they held no official ties to any other Indian group, they also indicated that they represented a large majority of tribal members when they lent their support to the CIA bill, H.R. 4918.

Ultimately, the only group in support of S. 1442 remained the tribal council, the authors of the bill. Furthermore, immediately prior to the hearings in Spokane, the council had unanimously passed a resolution in opposition of the CIA bill, H.R. 4918. The opposition groups pointed to this state of affairs as a reflection of the council's lack of connection with tribal members. The CIA and its members continually referred to the council as corrupt puppets of a corrupt Indian Bureau, and cited this as a reason to support termination. The council refuted CIA and CLP claims that they did not comprehend tribal members' needs and reminded tribal members of the special subcommittee they had impaneled to study termination options. Group leaders held meetings in each of the four tribal districts—Omak, Nespelem, Keller, and Inchelium—so that tribal members could share their opinions. Critics called these meetings a joke and asserted that the group leaders and the council refused to allow the people to participate.[2]

The 1963 subcommittee hearings would be the first public hearings held on Colville termination. The tribal council had limited previous reservation meetings to tribal members only (with the exception of Congressman Walt Horan), because those hearings were not to be part of the public record. The 1963 hearings were initiated by the subcommittee to hear public comment on S. 1442, which necessarily required Colvilles to broaden the discourse. The Subcommittee on Indian Affairs subsequently held four more sets of hearings on Colville termination, and the progress and changes in the arguments provide insight into how tribal members learned the rules of debate and also how their opinions on termination changed as the years progressed.

The tribal council submitted S. 1442, which was essentially H.R. 8469 plus the BIA's suggested amendments. H.R. 8469 had died in the previous congressional session, and the council updated it for resubmission in 1963. Assistant secretary of the Interior John Carver, Jr., summarized the council's position:

> The Colville Business Council's basic premise that there is a need for a two-phased program for accomplishing the termination of the Federal trust over their affairs was influenced by the fact that they went to the Klamath country in the course of their study, and drew some cogent empirical conclusions from the experiences of the Klamath Indians. ... In short, they feel that if they can offer the membership a planned economy that has reasonable prospects for success, and if the members have sufficient time to understand and thoroughly assess the economic

alternatives, a more prudent decision will be reached and a more whole-some and viable community attained. Hence, their proposal that they be enabled statutorily to plan first, then offer the legislation to imple-ment the plan, and terminate the Federal trust by the enactment of the terms of that plan.[3]

During the hearing, the council asserted that they had tried to obtain the opinions of tribal members. Councilman Joe Boyd, a member of the Lakes band, told the subcommittee about the council's efforts to talk to tribal members. Thirty-eight group leaders were appointed from nine-teen districts to lead discussions on Colville termination. These districts encompassed not only the reservation but also cities off the reservation, such as Spokane and Seattle, and other towns where sizable Colville pop-ulations lived. Colville tribal members attended these meetings to try to gain a more complete understanding of termination as well as to form their own responses to termination. The council also mailed approxi-mately two thousand surveys, to all adult members of the tribe. A total of 1,250 members completed the first poll, and 1,066 completed the sec-ond poll. Once the council and group leaders analyzed the information they had collected, they composed S. 1442. The tribal council approved S. 1442 by a majority of six to five at a special session in August of 1963. Tribal council chairman Harvey Moses acknowledged:

> The issue before us is a grave issue, involving a vast area . . . to which our members attach a great deal of sentiment, in that our forefathers had to suffer a great deal of humiliation and deprivation in order to retain this reservation for us. Before we jeopardize our present status we must take into consideration to the fullest extent all of the problems that may arise and cause regret due to hasty action.[4]

A multitude of steps had to be completed prior to removal of fed-eral supervision. Tribal members who believed that surveys of natural and human resources, including forest, mineral, and hunting rights, as well as medical care and other services, could be concluded in six months had no comprehension of the number of people and organiza-tions involved in those steps. Those who favored a per capita distribution of assets deemed that solution the easiest to execute, but in reality it would likely have proved equally as complex as the remaining option, and the payments would not have been dispersed in any rapid fashion. S. 1442 tried to address as many issues of concern to tribal members as possible, including guarantees for law and order from the state comparable to what the tribes had received from the federal government, and post-termination protection of fishing and hunting rights. The council also wanted to protect surface and subsurface water rights and usage rights, as well as obtain promises for improved roads and sanitation, and school and hospital construction. Tax protection remained tremendously important because tribal members did not pay county taxes on trust lands and rejected the principle of taxation. The council feared that tribal members would suffer similar fates as some Menominees, who had recently liquidated large parcels of the land they gained through termination in order to pay their income and property taxes. Further, in the event of a cash payment for liquidation, the council wanted that amount to remain exempt from income tax. Council members requested a provision for education and training for tribal members prior to withdrawal, so that Colvilles would be comfortable managing their own financial and practical affairs.

The business council tried to learn from the experiences of the Menominee and Klamath terminations and to avoid similar mistakes. Chairman Moses cited the several visits the council and the termination subcommittee paid to Klamath country and how they had observed "firsthand the inequities of converting vast and valuable resources to an unrestricted status, while running the gauntlet of complex transitions." The business council determined that such short-range decisions ultimately proved shortsighted and that a poorly considered plan caused the Klamaths to be back in court with the US government almost immediately following termination.[5]

At the October 24 subcommittee on Indian Affairs hearing in Spokane, Dr. Paschal Sherman of the Petitioners Party interpreted the government's call for termination in another way. He reminded the subcommittee that while the Colvilles had to submit a termination bill, P.L. 772 did not actually require that they terminate. The Petitioners Party represented about four hundred tribal members who either had farms on the reservation or held employment there on a regular basis. As such, the party believed that they had a more pertinent interest in the termination proceedings because they would be among the tribal members most directly affected by termination. Members of the Petitioners Party first vocalized the opinion that people who chose to live away from the reservation had already been terminated: "They have withdrawn; the government has nothing to do or say about how they make their living."[6]

With tribal members hopelessly divided on the issue of termination, Sherman feared that the government would ultimately have to make the final decision, so he had proposed his national park alternative. Sherman indicated that he had already received favorable feedback on his proposal from the Interior Department and from the president's Council of Economic Advisors, and he offered the solution as a way for Congress to deal with other tribes as well. He wanted the Colville Reservation to be officially included in the president's program "so that in the future neither Congress nor the government will be actively urging termination."[7] Because federal dollars would be spent, Sherman considered termination a public policy and consequently argued that the reservation should become a public and recreational place for everyone, not just for Colvilles.

Several vocal members of the Colville Indian Association attended the hearings as well, primarily to attack the council's termination bill. The CIA had two major arguments with S. 1442: the tribal council had not held a referendum to determine what kind of termination tribal members desired; and the two-step process that it proposed did not actually terminate federal oversight but instead extended it indefinitely. The CIA proposed an alternative, H.R. 4918, "to provide members of the Colville Confederated Tribes with full citizenship rights by extinguishing the tribal entity and vesting each tribal member with his equal cash share of the fair market value of all reservation assets of the Colville Confederated Tribes in the State of Washington."[8]

H.R. 4918 called for appraisals of tribal assets and a closing of the rolls within six months after Congress enacted the bill, not the day Congress enacted it, as required in S. 1442. Closing the rolls remained a sensitive topic among tribal members, most of whom did not want the rolls closed at all. Closing the rolls meant that no one in the future could be added as a member of the Colville Tribes, even a child born one minute after the deadline. Some tribal members who favored termination also wanted the flexibility to include new family members on the tribal rolls. The tribal council had investigated submitting a bill that did not include a roll closure, only to be told by Congress that it would categorically reject any such bill. A bill that did not include a roll-closure provision meant that new tribal members could continue to be recognized or added to the rolls, which would effectively nullify termination of federal recognition.

Everyone on the roll would receive an equal distribution of tribal assets, with minors' shares held in trust. H.R. 4918 called for a referendum on the proposed termination plan and required 60 percent of tribal members voting in the election to approve it. In 1963 no one objected to the language of the voting requirement, but it would become a deal breaker in later years. Because Indians often express disapproval through silence, it is likely that this silence would extend to the ballot box. Indians would interpret a refusal to vote as opposition to the person or initiative up for consideration. If a considerable portion of eligible Colville voters refused to vote on termination, the results from a vote would represent not a true majority Colville opinion but only a majority opinion among those Colvilles who voted. When the BIA refused to approve any termination bill not passed by 60 percent of eligible voters, the Colville Indian Association pointed to that position as another example of the bureau interfering in tribal business.

The CIA bill also differed from the council bill in its requirement that the Interior Department assess the value of the tribe's hunting and fishing rights. CIA members wanted the sum of that value represented in the total compensation that tribal members would receive. After the enactment date, tribal members would no longer have their guaranteed treaty rights to hunt and fish in the "usual and accustomed places." Most CIA members lived off the reservation and did not value the hunting and fishing rights to any great degree, but residents of the reservation still depended upon game and fish to fill their tables. Most reservation residents survived on an average income of less than $1,800 a year, and venison, elk, and salmon kept them fed throughout the year.

The proposed CIA bill's requirement for valuation and payment for cessation of hunting and fishing rights illustrates how clearly and cleanly the CIA wished to sever the Colville-federal relationship. No rights or recognition of previous rights would exist after the enactment of the bill. Section 15 of the bill definitively called for publication of the Federal Register, declaring that the trust relationship had been terminated and that "Indian status shall no longer be applicable to the members of the tribe."[9]

On the first day of the first subcommittee hearings regarding Colville termination in Spokane, so many tribal members attended that the committee had to ask people to mail in their statements because there was not enough time to hear everyone's testimony. With a dozen members heard that day, the CIA and its supporters offered the most united front, but each tribal member offered perceptive observations about the legislation facing them. Colville Indian Association member Helen Toulou, of the Lakes band, asked why she should pass S. 1442 when it would put her back one hundred years. "I don't need their protection any longer. . . . In everything, we live modern. We don't use feathers, buckskins or anything. We don't dwell in teepees with campfires. We are absolutely as modern as you are." Toulou craved the end of the Colvilles' special designation and wanted to become "part of the [American] Nation."[10]

Many CIA members contended that tribal members lacked full citizenship rights because the Bureau of Indian Affairs still had control over individual lease income and had to approve tribal expenditures, such as per capita and judgment payments. One member charged that the Indian did not enjoy the rights or protections afforded true US citizens. Ronald Nelson insisted that each tribal member had a moral obligation to perform in becoming a member of the United States. Nelson opposed S. 1442 because it would prevent true citizenship and not allow tribal members to attain rights other Americans enjoyed. "It seems that we are American citizens away from the reservation, but our property held in trust is not subject to the protection of the laws of the white man."[11]

Mary Sumerlin, a CIA trustee from Keller and member of the San Poil–Lakes bands, railed against S. 1442 because it did not uphold the requirements of P.L. 772, the bill that reinstated the 818,000-acre North Half in return for the Colville Tribes drafting termination legislation:

We are strongly opposed to S. 1442 because it was prepared by the Indian Bureau for its own purposes and because it dishonestly parades as a termination bill; because it dishonestly parades the vestment of property interests as meaningful when the Commissioner of Indian Affairs has already told some of our members that such interests are intangible; which says to us that this bill would settle upon us a worthless paper economy while the substance of our assets would disappear forever. S. 1442 will not solve the so-called Indian problem, nor the problem of the Indian people, but would actually aggravate them.[12]

Several tribal members called on the subcommittee to favor H.R. 4918 so that they could cash out their shares and invest their money as they wanted. Martha Johnson called this "economic liberty" and said that S. 1442 did not provide for it. "We [the CIA] strongly oppose S. 1442 on the grounds that it is designed to delay the time when we can participate in forming the course our own future is to take."[13]

Violet Assing brought up the issue of welfare and how allotments and trust holdings affected tribal members who needed assistance. In the current welfare system, people who wanted to apply for state aid had to dispose of their surplus property—that is, anything that could be converted to capital—before they could establish need. Because many tribal members held allotments or interests in allotments, they had to first get the BIA's permission to sell their property. The process was always a lengthy one and was worse when more than one person held shares in an allotment. Since many allotments dated back sixty years or more, multiple owners or heirs of one allotment was the norm. Assing's concern was that too many tribal members lived meanly, yet the state still considered them property owners because they held fractional shares (one-quarter of one-quarter acre, for example) in an allotment and as a consequence did not qualify for aid. For her, H.R. 4918, not S. 1442, was a way for tribal members in need to develop a healthy standard of living and not be victims of poverty any longer.[14] Norma Inks saw the irony of the termination process: "As strange as it seems, the dissolution of the ties which bind us to a government hostile to us in particular cannot be achieved without the consent of the United States. . . . S. 1442 is purposefully and carefully designed to strengthen, perpetuate and nationalize arbitrary powers parading in the name of a government hostile to all U.S. citizens, and infringing upon both the civil liberties and property rights of U.S. citizen Indians."[15]

While not all tribal members testifying in opposition to S. 1442 perceived the council as a hostile bunch, many did not agree with the council's perceptions of or their goals for the tribe. Sybil Berglund averred, "We do not want to be, as Harvey Moses, council chairman, stated at the general meeting in Nespelem, 'a little nation of our own with its own laws.' We do not want this separate autocratic and socialistic substitution of Bureau rule superseding Constitutional rights."[16]

In contrast to the many members who opposed S. 1442 because it did not offer a one-step termination plan, Louie Wapato, kin to Paschal

Sherman, opposed S. 1442 because he opposed termination itself. He spoke on behalf of the 462 tribal members in the Petitioners Party: "To our way of thinking, these bills represent a question of life and death for the tribes." Citing Kennedy's promise to deal in a straightforward manner with the people his agencies serve, he said, "S. 1442 is clearly in conflict with the present administration's position on Indian affairs, which was announced and published as 'development with no termination.'" Wapato explained to the committee that his cohort resided and worked on the reservation—whether in grazing, agriculture, or other employment. He agreed with Sherman's assessment that "the private party" members who sought passage of H.R. 4918 had already terminated. "They have ceased to be members of the tribe, and their corporate or other associated existence is private and has no sovereignty. They are under state law and therefore legally bound to leave the tribes alone."[17]

While the first day of hearings hosted a full house of tribal members waiting to share their thoughts on termination—some who lived in the Spokane area and some who had traveled from the reservation—even more tribal members attended the Nespelem hearings the following day. The paved and unpaved lots around the Colville Indian Agency buildings overflowed with cars and pickups as tribal members traveled from across the reservation to give their testimony on this heated topic. The meeting on October 25 began with testimony from state senator Wilbur Hallauer, whose district included the Colville Reservation. The senator clearly intended his remarks to be a positive representation of the Colvilles, but he cloaked them in such offensive language that it was difficult to tell whether he supported or opposed this constituency:

> We have got to look at the question in terms of overall philosophy of whether they are yet ready to graduate from the ranks of the reserva-tion. . . . I have come to the conclusion that a considerable majority of the people are now ready to leave the "diaper stage" that the reservation imposes upon them. . . . I think we can draw a parallel between the circum-stances of the Negro people in the United States since their emancipation and the reservation structure as a means, a stepping stone, between a primitive culture and a modern culture. The Negro people today still have their Uncle Toms. They still have their Old Massa's. I say it is time the Uncle Toms were put in the background and it is time the Old Massa's, in this case the Bureau of Indian Affairs, went into the cold ground.[18]

At that point, an unidentified tribal member stood and asserted that the senator did not have a right to join the meeting and tell them what to do. In response to both the dissatisfied tribal member and Senator Hallauer, council chairman Harvey Moses added, "The state senator commented that the Colvilles should arrange to get out of the diaper stage and that H.R. 4918 would be the probable cure-all. At this time, I would like to disagree, for he is not familiar with all our problems."[19]

Councilman Frank George opposed termination in any form and offered his testimony on behalf of many of the full-bloods and others who closely followed Indian traditions. They especially viewed termination legislation unfavorably, he said.

> "Liquidation" of tribal assets, "termination" of Federal trusteeship, and "emancipating" the Indians all mean the same thing and these words serve as catchwords for those who would like to relieve the Indians from their remaining property by depriving the Indians of the promised Federal protection now accorded them. Any termination of Federal trusteeship will be detrimental to the membership of the Confederated Tribe of the Colville Reservation. The withdrawal of Federal trusteeship will jeopardize the economic welfare of many Indians, especially those of the older generations who do not fully understand the ways of life that were not of their devising. . . . These full-blood Indians have been on the receiving end of the most fallacious judgments. There is much misunderstanding of the Indian due to the fact that many non-Indians and also mixed bloods are prone to appraise the Indians' society, Indian culture, and Indian religion by white standards. These people who choose to sit in judgment on the Indians are themselves very conspicuously lacking in the true spiritual depth and the profound ethical traditions observed by the descendants of the first inhabitants of the North American continent.[20]

The government had a responsibility to Indians, he argued, since the executive branch of the government had created the Colville Confederacy. George castigated the liquidators and the terminationists who "possess a small quantum of Indian blood, but who are very vocal in claiming a large degree of privilege as Indians." George acknowledged his minority position on the council to the subcommittee and also expressed his alarm at the council's pro-termination stance. Councilman Steve Cleveland echoed George's dismay about the termination legislation, especially because no tribal referendum had occurred before the creation of S. 1442.[21] The council had moved to kill or extinguish the tribe, he charged, and the body had been empowered to do so with the advent of federal termination policy.

The anti-terminationists raised their voices throughout the morning. T. B. Charley, chair of the Petitioners Party and member of the Methow band, spoke of the reservation as a homeland and said that his group wanted to hold on to the reservation so that it could represent the same values to their children and grandchildren. Charley wanted to focus on development and conservation of reservation resources, for their own use as well as to protect future generations, "but, mostly, because it is our home," he said. He recognized the motivation of the pro-termination group, because he agreed with Wapato and Sherman that these Colvilles had in effect already terminated. Terminationists estimated that each enrolled member would receive $30,000 to $40,000 once Congress enacted the termination act. "It is hard for us—it would be hard for anyone—to resist the idea of receiving that much money out of a clear sky," he said. Tribal members had not proven that they were interested in investing or planning with their money, he said, but seemed to be focused only in satisfying that moment's needs. Tribal income had exceeded twenty million dollars collectively in twenty years, but most tribal members had little to show for it. "We cannot expect these people to be investment minded now. The money would be squandered and soon most of the people would be buried in a junk pile of Cadillacs."[22]

Charley presented the subcommittee with a report of the council's termination planning committee's visit to Klamath country and their findings of the post-termination mood and conditions there. The committee had spoken with both terminated and remaining members, as well as officials chosen to manage the Klamath's remaining resources. One remaining member, Dibbon Cook, reportedly felt generally satisfied with his situation and remained comfortable under trust officer control, but he did acknowledge his fear that young people who were about to come of age would choose to liquidate so they could "buy new cars and otherwise keep up with their terminated friends." L. Q. Moore, a Klamath who had chosen to liquidate and who took some credit in seeking the termination of the Klamath tribe, offered a different perspective. He believed that termination had been a good thing for his people, although he indicated that some members suffered without the services and protections offered by the reservation. He managed his $43,000 well and believed that if others did not, they had created their own misfortune.[23] At a meeting with a group of Klamath members who had consistently opposed termination, the Colville committee listened as they blamed lack of unity among tribal members for the undoing of the Klamath tribe. "Complete unity is the only way to avoid complete termination," they advised.[24]

The Colville delegation also met with Wayne Blair, the Klamath's trust officer. The group met Blair at the bank, where he surmised that as many as 50 percent of the withdrawing members had spent all of their money in just over a year, and very few of them had assets to justify the expenditures. Family members supported others who had spent their money, and while no adults had registered on the county welfare rolls to date, Blair anticipated that many would soon have to.[25] Prior to termination, Klamath tribal members could seek assistance from the tribe, camp on tribal land, and hunt for sustenance. Now that the tribe no longer existed and had no land base or social services to offer, Klamath Indians would have to seek help from non-Indian county services.

At the Nespelem meeting, Harris Thomas also spoke on behalf of the Petitioners Party, and he imagined a parallel to the Klamath experience. He deemed the Colville Reservation as one of the best in the country, and praised its cultural significance as well as the occasional monetary reward enjoyed from per capitas and other payments. "Now it is proposed to turn it over to people who will run it into the ground within a few short years. We know our people. They do not have the education and experience to run big business." He reminded the committee of the Klamath remark on the importance for the Colvilles in being united in their approach to termination. "In my lifetime we have never been united on any major issues. Look at us now." He asked for the continuation of federal supervision because he believed that the Colvilles had been doing quite well under it.[26]

Thomas further contended, "Nothing less than disaster will befall my people upon the termination of Federal supervision over their affairs at this time." He cited the tribal members' educational levels in 1961: 283 high school graduates, 37 college graduates, and 23 with no schooling. Of the college graduates, most of them lived off the reservation, and 43 percent of those graduates indicated that they would not return to live on the reservation if termination occurred instead of development of tribal resources. Although many terminationists presumed that all members living off the reservation had become economically better off than reservation residents, Thomas produced compelling numbers of urban tribal members on welfare rolls. He explained the dichotomy this way: "Indians with relatives seldom starve." In other words, Colvilles on the reservation could survive on the land and with the aid of their families. Without the land base, families would scatter and subsistence hunting and fishing would not be possible. Welfare and its attendant requirements troubled him greatly. He feared that reservation tribal members would not be able to hold on to their money. Lacking job training, they would need to turn to welfare. First, they would have to liquidate their property. "Aside from the threat of losing [the lands] in the courts to schemers," Thomas said, "in consideration of the age brackets of title holders, they stand a good chance of being forced to sell their lands for debts or as a condition for obtaining state assistance."[27]

Several of the same Colville Indian Association members who addressed the group in Spokane also spoke in Nespelem. Local non-Indian residents and officials from towns adjacent to the reservation had come to voice their near unanimous support of Colville termination. Ruth Scofield, of the Oroville Chamber of Commerce, believed that the Colvilles had been denied a choice in their own future. "In September," she said, "President Kennedy told the United Nations, 'People of the world must be free to choose their own future.' If this precept is right for people behind the Iron Curtain it should also apply to people behind the buckskin curtain."[28]

Suzette Costain, a member of the Lakes band from Inchelium, spoke about her past and her future and strongly expressed her opinion of all termination legislation: "We want our money for Grand Coulee Dam and for Chief Joseph Dam. Before we do anything more. I am going to hold on to my reservation because if the guys are not going to pay us for any of that, it is no use selling any more." She guessed she would have to pick grapes all her life in order to survive, because she could not count on the BIA to follow through with its promises and agreements.[29] In the Colville Tribes' history of dealings with the BIA and the US government, they had not been paid for land or mineral sales on five major occasions. The willingness of tribal members seeking termination to believe that the government would pay any price, much less the correct price, remains baffling in light of previous events.

The Colville Liquidation Promoters' statement of termination focused on identity within the Colville Tribes:

> The term *tribe*, using the dictionary meaning of "group of people united by race and customs under the same leaders," when applied to the Colville Confederated Tribes is a misnomer, for by no stretch of the imagination can the people who today comprise the entity known as the Colville Confederated Tribes be likened to a "group of people united by race and customs." The only common bond uniting people of this entity is the ownership in common of the Colville Indian Reservation and assets. . . . The different bands who originally composed the membership of the Colville Confederated Tribes have never had a common relationship and have refused full acceptance of each other as would be characteristic of a true Indian tribe.[30]

The liquidation promoters used this assertion in concert with the figure of 75 percent of the adult population choosing to reside off the reservation as justification for terminating the federal relationship.

Members from both sides of the termination debate made salient points, and both positions were equally represented. Mary Nicholson of Tonasket told the committee, "I am for terminating Federal supervision and liquidating all of our assets, and the sooner we do it the better off we will be. We do not want to remain wards of the government. . . . I have raised ten orphan brothers and sisters on my own. And I have put them through school. I feel that I am quite capable of handling my own affairs."[31] Louis Covington offered a countering sentiment. "I think liquidation at this time should not be considered because it doesn't take into consideration those who don't have the background to cope with the situation and the loss of their homes."[32]

Tribal member John Cleveland agreed with Covington. He spoke on behalf of several farmers and cattlemen he knew and indicated their worries about operating without the same modern equipment and means that white farmers and ranchers used. He feared that Colvilles would suffer from this disadvantage if Congress removed federal supervision. "I think I am the most privileged citizen who walks in the United States of America. I have the same privileges as anybody else, but am not forced to pay taxes like them, and even so, I still do not make a good living." Cleveland believed that termination was inevitable, but he hoped that the Colvilles would resist as long as possible. "My people were promised when we moved onto these lands; it will be yours as long as you want to keep it, the State of Washington and other outside governments will not interfere with your internal affairs. Well, Federal policies have changed and in due time we are going to be turned loose."[33]

The privileges that Cleveland valued came under attack at the hearings in Seattle. Edward Thompson of the Colville Indian Association decried them as preventing Colvilles from advancing into the modern world. Viola Fisher echoed Thompson's remarks and asserted that special laws for one group provided inequity for all: "The days of the wide open spaces are past: we are looking forward with the rest of America to the outer spaces. We want to put our buckskins, our moccasins, our beaded gloves and feathered headdresses in the museums where they belong—where all other much-treasured remnants of our colorful history are kept."[34]

The Colvilles, Fisher told the subcommittee, should refuse to be guilty of the moral cowardice she associated with special rights. She craved equality and felt especially stung when her supervisor at Boeing, upon learning that she would attend the committee hearings, asked if she would dress differently than normal. He imagined that she would wear a buckskin dress and moccasins to address other Colvilles at the meeting. Fisher believed that remaining an Indian would only continue to invite embarrassing and often hurtful assumptions. Virginia DeCamp had also been wounded by discrimination, but at the hands of other Colvilles. She protested that, although she possessed only one-eighth Colville blood, resided in the city, and was married to a white man, she still felt connected to Indian customs. She said she would like to live on the reservation but considered the reservation Utopia. One could not live in Utopia, she protested. Those who accused the urban Colville members of only being interested in money angered her, and she claimed her respect for other tribal members: "As for the old people, I honor them as much as anyone else, and I feel that if they can live their last few years with a little bit of pleasure, it is better."[35]

All Seattle speakers in favor of termination raised the issue of special rights, equality, and civil rights. Helene Foster suggested that if the tribal members and the committee could not create a workable termination solution, then they should contact Robert Kennedy, attorney general of the United States:

> Right now we are very much concerned with civil rights and President Kennedy has offered equal opportunity for all. We are hopeful that this includes the American Indian as well as the Negro. I feel that if we cannot get equal opportunity and full civil rights that then we should refer our case to the Justice Department, Robert Kennedy. He has been very busy helping the Negroes and perhaps he would like to help us.[36]

Each participant at the hearings took the process seriously. They invoked the president and the attorney general sincerely, as sympathetic men who might be able to offer a more workable solution than termination. The preparation of testimony and the public nature of presenting it must have been arduous. Most tribal members, especially those who spoke only in one of the Colville dialects, had little experience in public speaking. Many confessed to being nervous and asked the committee for reassurance about their testimony. They wrote letters and contributed written statements, and many who testified also pled their case to various BIA officials. The Colville Indian Association made sure that their position paper and bylaws would be included in the appendix, so that subcommittee members could review them after the meetings. Tribal members recognized the import of these hearings, learned the rules of participating in the hearings, and wanted their names and opinions on the record for this debate. It was an unfamiliar process, but one that tribal members embraced.

The tribal council, after hearing so much testimony from tribal members in favor of a one-step termination process, amended S. 1442 to reflect tribal members' wishes. The Senate subcommittee passed S. 1442 in August 1963, but the bill died at the end of the congressional session because the House did not have time to act upon it.

The 1963 hearings set the stage for later hearings. Different tribal members would participate in the 1965 hearings, and the arguments would change and solidify, then change again. The Colvilles continued to try to answer so many questions for themselves. Who are we? Who deserves to be counted? Why do we want this? Why are outsiders doing this to us?

Among the most interesting questions, though, are: Why did the Colvilles press for termination even as every day brought more information on how that policy had so badly affected the Klamath and the Menominee? Why did the battle remain so important to the groups who wanted it? And how much more vocal did termination opponents become as they learned more about other termination experiences? Many of these questions remain unanswerable, but we can find some indications in the hearings that followed.

ELECTION

BUSINESS COUNCIL MEMBERS

SATURDAY, MAY 11

ATTENTION, TRIBAL MEMBERS

(So the public and Congress can know and act on our views)

IF YOU ARE AGAINST:

- BIA TASK FORCE POLICIES
- LONG RANGE DEVELOPMENT POLICIES
- BENEFITS TO ONLY FEW TRIBAL MEMBERS
- INCORPORATION OF TRIBAL ASSETS

- BUSINESS COUNCIL SYSTEM
- REDUCTION IN CASH VALUE OF MEMBERS' SHARES
- MORE EXPENDITURES — SMALLER PER CAPITAS
- TRIBAL MONEY INVESTED IN LAND PURCHASE PROGRAM

AND IF YOU ARE FOR:

- TERMINATION
- LIQUIDATION
- REFERENDUM ON TERMINATION
- AN END TO BUSINESS COUNCIL SYSTEM

- EQUAL FULL FAIR MARKET VALUE SHARE PAID TO ALL MEMBERS
- EQUAL CHANCE FOR INVESTMENTS AND EDUCATION FOR ALL MEMBERS

VOTE FOR PLEDGED LIQUIDATION CANDIDATES

OMAK DISTRICT
- ☒ Narcisse Nicholson, Jr.
- ☒ Caroline F. Waggoner.

NESPELEM DISTRICT
- ☒ Donna Lee Palmanteer
- ☒ James II. Gallaher

KELLER DISTRICT
- ☒ Barney Rickard

INCHELIUM DISTRICT
(No pledged candidates)

Candidates endorsed by independent non-affiliated boosters for Liquidation — Colville Liquidation Promoters, Box 171, Omak, Wash.

Colville Liquidation Promoters Poster, ca. 1963. Source: Senate Committee on Interior and Insular Affairs, Subcommittee on Indian Affairs, S. 1442, S. 1169, 88th Congress, 1st sess., October 24-26, 1963, p. 209.

COLVILLE LIQUIDATION PROMOTERS
P. O. Box 171, Omak, Washington   FRES.- Ruby S. Babcook
   April 19, 1963   VICE-.RES.- Ira H. Lum
                                               SEC.-TREAS.- Alice K. Huber
Dear Member of the Colville Confederated Tribes:

          The kind of Termination Act Congress gives us can possibly mean either
that a FULL FAIR MARKET VALUE share of the reservation assets could be paid to us
OR that the reservation assets could be put under a tribal corporation with the
tribal members being shareholders. In the case of a tribal corporation, the value
of each share could be based on the ECONOMIC VALUE of the reservation assets or
about only 20% (twenty per cent) of it's FAIR MARKET VALUE. The corporation could
control HOW, WHEN and IF the reduced shares would be paid.

          As examples — the Klamath Tribe of Oregon had a FULL SHARE, FAIR MARKET
VALUE type of termination with tribal members being paid on that basis. The Menominee Tribe of Wisconsin had an ECONOMIC VALUE type of termination. They were
not paid cash but were given a bond of reduced value with restrictions against
cashing the bond.

          When Congress SOON considers the type of termination that WE SHOULD
HAVE they will need to know how YOU feel about the long range development programs
that the Bureau of Indian Affairs and the Colville Business Council are putting
us under. YOU KNOW whether or not you and your children have any interest in such
programs and if YOU could do better with your FULL SHARE of reservation assets.

          What do these points have to do with the ELECTION for Business Council
members this year? We, the Colville Liquidation Promoters (an independent organization), are supporting those candidates who have PUBLICLY PLEDGED their intention
to work towards termination and liquidation. We intend to prove to Congress
BY THE ELECTION RESULTS that most of the people of this tribe EXPECT a FULL SHARE,
FAIR MARKET VALUE type of termination by liquidation of the reservation assets
that they own in common (together). Allotments are not included.

          YOUR VOTE IS IMPORTANT! If you do not plan to drive to your district
polling place BE SURE TO SEND FOR AN ABSENTEE BALLOT IMMEDIATELY. YOUR BALLOT
WILL HAVE TO BE POSTMARKED NO LATER THAN THE ELECTION DAY WHICH IS MAY 11th.
ASK FOR A BALLOT FOR THE DISTRICT IN WHICH YOU LIVE, HAVE LIVED BEFORE, ARE
ALLOTED OR LIVE NEAREST. EITHER NESPELEM, OMAK, KELLER OR INCHELIUM DISTRICT.
YOU CANNOT VOTE IN MORE THAN ONE DISTRICT. A recent move by you, less than a
year ago, would mean that you vote in your former district.
For your convenience in sending for your ABSENTEE BALLOT, use form below.
Cut off on dotted line, fill in and mail directly to Nespelem, Wash.
Be sure to SIGN YOUR NAME AND ADDRESS.
-

Mr. Harry Owhi, Executive Secretary,   Date_____
Colville Confederated Tribes,
Nespelem, Washington

          Please send to me immediately an absentee ballot for voting in the
1963 election for members to the Colville Business Council. The district that
I vote in is_____

                              Signed by,

                              Member Colville Confederated Tribes
                              Address

Colville Liquidation Promoters Campaign Letter, ca. 1963. Source: Senate
Committee on Interior and Insular Affairs, Subcommittee on Indian Affairs,
S. 1442, S. 1169, 88th Congress, 1st sess., October 24-26, 1963, p. 210.

CANDIDATES PLATFORM

To the members of the Colville Confederated Tribes:

We, the undersigned, being candidates in the 1963 election for members of the Business Council of the Colville Confederated Tribes, declare that if we are elected we will work towards the termination of federal supervision and liquidation of the assets of the Colville Confederated Tribes at fair market value with the distribution of an equal share to each enrolled member of the Tribes. We consider this to be the best way to promote and protect the interests of the Colville Indians and to improve the economic condition of the Indians and their posterity.

OMAK DISTRICT, Signed by:

(Frieda) Cardine Raymond Waggoner

Maxie Nicholson Jr.

NESPELEM DISTRICT, Signed by:

Dennis M. Palmanteer

Jamie H. Gallaher

INCHELIUM DISTRICT, Signed by:

(No pledged candidate)

(No pledged candidate)

KELLER DISTRICT, Signed by:

Henry Packard

Candidates endorsed by Colville Liquidation Promoters, Box 171, Omak, Wash.

Candidates were selected from among those who had filed for candidacy and have been certified. None of the three certified candidates in the Inchelium District qualified as liquidation supporters.

Colville Liquidation Promoters Platform, ca. 1963. Source: Senate Committee on Interior and Insular Affairs, Subcommittee on Indian Affairs, S. 1442, S. 1169, 88th Congress, 1st sess., October 24-26, 1963, p. 211.

FOREST SOUTH OF CACHE CREEK ROAD BETWEEN NESPELEM AND KELLER

CHAPTER 4

"What is their future?"

A POWER struggle for control of termination dialogue and the termination debate continued to rage on the Colville Reservation. Questions of whether the tribe should terminate as well as how their termination goals should be accomplished seemed to permeate every aspect of tribal life. By 1965 the overwhelming majority of tribal members who favored termination wanted a one-step process: they wanted Congress to approve termination, then cut each tribal member a check for the value of the Colville land and resources. Those who favored termination had a louder collective voice and had won additional seats on the tribal council, but those who opposed it held firm and continued to argue that the government must honor its obligations. That spring and summer, the Subcommittee on Indian Affairs held two sets of hearings on Colville termination in Washington, DC, before returning to the state of Washington in November.

The subcommittee was now considering two bills, both of which provided for termination of the Colville Indians and the Colville Reservation. The bills did differ in their approach to termination. H.R. 5925, introduced at the behest of the Colville Business Council by Tom Foley of Washington State,[1] provided for one-step termination of federal supervision over the property and the tribal members, but also included a remaining option for those tribal members who did not wish to terminate. This bill, which was almost identical to the Klamath termination bill, reflected the wishes of the majority of the Colville membership involved in the termination debate. H.R. 6331, introduced by Thomas Pelly, also of Washington State, and sponsored by the Colville Indian Association, provided tribal members with full ownership and vested members with equal cash shares representing the equity of all reservation assets; it did not include an option to remain.[2]

Congressman Walt Horan, who had introduced previous termination bills for the Colvilles, had angered the president of the Colville Liquidation Promoters, Ruby Babcock. In 1964 he had told her that he still favored a two-step termination plan for the Colvilles and indicated that they should work through the council to design such a plan. Babcock observed that the majority of the council now favored a one-step plan and that Horan constantly made "reference to the Indians as though they still lived in the days of chiefs."[3] Babcock must have been pleased when Foley defeated Horan in the Fifth Congressional District race in 1965.

While the bills differed in the level of termination proposed, in 1965 they both contained a one-step termination process, which diverged from the two-step approach the business council had originally suggested in 1963. The council endeavored to reflect the wishes of tribal members when it wrote H.R. 5925. A primary reason for this change in approach from the business council lay in the new composition of the council members. The council elections in May 1965 strengthened the hold of pro-terminationists. True to their word, the Colville Liquidation Promoters ran for tribal council and several won. The biggest change that year came in the displacement of Harvey Moses as tribal chairman. He had held the post for eight years, but the new CLP council members joined forces with the independents on the council and voted in a new chairman, Narcisse Nicholson Jr. of the Colville Liquidation Promoters.[4] This new leadership group held a ten-to-four majority in favor of termination.

Many flaws existed in both bills, but the appraisal clause and the voting requirements were of primary concern to the subcommittee. The bills provided for appraisals of land and resources only after tribal members voted to accept termination and after Congress had enacted the bill. The voting requirement, the first step toward attaining termination, required the approval of only 60 percent of tribal members voting on termination legislation to pass, but did not include a requirement for passage by a majority of tribal members eligible to vote. Tribal members and Congress members alike objected to the voting requirement, and many tribal members spoke out forcefully against being required to vote for termination before Congress committed to a dollar amount for their reservation's resources. The question of hunting and fishing rights remained a significant issue throughout the hearings; most tribal members had great concern about how those would be assigned a monetary value, and reservation tribal members wondered whether they would retain those rights if the Colvilles terminated.

In April tribal members traveled to Washington, DC, to testify on S. 1413. The majority members of the business council spoke in favor of it, indicating that a one-step process represented the needs and desires of the tribal members. The minority members of the council testified against S. 1413, and Joe Boyd indicated that tribal members should be aware of the value of the shares before voting to terminate. The *Tribal Tribune* reported that "some of the members of the minority group" questioned whether tribal members with a lesser blood degree or who resided far from the reservation had the right to participate in a tribal referendum about termination.[5]

Secretary of the Interior Stewart Udall agreed with the fundamentals of Foley's bill, but he noted that the Interior Department wanted it amended to require passage of a tribal referendum on termination by a majority of tribal members eligible to vote. A native of Arizona, Udall had worked on several Arizona tribes' behalf as an attorney and had remained committed to Native American interests throughout his terms in Congress and the Interior Department. Udall also indicated that the Interior generally supported termination and the end of federal supervision, as long as it reflected tribal members' needs, but he opposed the payout option supported by the legislation. He noted the extensive poverty on the reservation and wondered whether a cash settlement would really help the Indians. "As a group of human beings, what are their characteristics? What are their problems? Will cash relieve them? If not, what is their future?"[6]

Udall believed that the lack of education and financial inexperience of many Colvilles would cause the Indians to run through a cash settlement quickly and ultimately have nothing to show for it. Instead, Udall proposed that the government help the Colvilles develop a forest products industry, while still terminating federal supervision if the Colvilles truly wished to sever the federal tie, and leave in place economic development resources that could help the Colvilles maintain a successful industry on their own. He cited the drain the Menominees placed on county assistance when their termination money ran out and business enterprises could not afford to offer assistance. First the county and then the state of Wisconsin had to step in and help them, and Udall did not want to replicate that financial situation for the Colvilles or for Washington State or the local counties.

Congressmen Foley and Mike E. Odell, in introducing their bills to the subcommittee, both asserted their belief that the majority of Colvilles supported termination, and that most either greatly participated in the non-Indian mainstream or would have no trouble adjusting to life as "nonsegregated" Americans. Odell further stated that the Indians he had talked to seemed "of a very high caliber and that the program of termination would be a great asset to them."[7] Subcommittee member Senator George Hansen of Idaho expressed a number of concerns related to both bills. In addition to wanting clarification on how the Klamaths had fared in their post-termination era, he also inquired after the Menominees. Senator John Race of Wisconsin noted that the Menominees currently operated at a $3.5 million deficit, and that many (former) reservation residents had spent all of their termination money in the last three and one half years. Senator Hansen wondered, "We set up these reservations for one purpose, as I understand it, to take care of them on a communal basis until they could take care of themselves. If we have not accomplished this purpose, it seems to me we are not ready to get out of business in this particular area."[8]

Senator James Haley, chair of the subcommittee, observed that the government had not yet done enough for Indians. "I think one of the blackest pages of American history has been the treatment of the American Indian." He noted that the government placed Indians in remote corners that offered barely more than subsistence living and provided little or no education or vocational opportunities. "We have encouraged the Indian to do nothing for himself. After seven or eight generations, he thinks he is not competent to get out in the world and he thinks of the reservation as his anchor." In consideration for the harm government paternalism had already done, Haley concluded, "We better proceed very cautiously in these matters, I think, and do the best we can."[9]

At the hearings in Washington, DC, Congressman Foley engaged Graham Holmes of the Bureau of Indian Affairs in a lengthy discussion about the voting amendment his office had proposed. Foley wondered why the bureau remained committed to that change when the tribal council had drafted the legislation to reflect only the opinions of those voting. Holmes explained, "Our suggestion is that a majority of adult members of the tribe get a full expression." Foley responded, "Is it not true that . . . those who are apathetic enough not to vote [would count] as negative votes. If enough people do not exercise the right to vote it fails?"[10]

Neither Foley nor Holmes understood the significance of voter participation on the reservation. Many Colvilles believed that the government had imposed its rules on them. Even though the Colvilles rejected the Indian Reorganization Act, their constitution is largely modeled on other tribal constitutions written by the BIA. Tribal nonparticipation in elections emerged less as a manifestation of apathy than as a statement against the institution of voting. When opposed to a person or an initiative, many tribal members simply refused to acknowledge the vote and did not participate. Barbara White Nicholson quoted an old Indian tradition, "The true Indian traditional way of showing dissension is by remaining silent."[11] Holmes did not realize that he protected this segment of the tribal population when he noted that the BIA would support the bill only if amended to reflect passage by a majority of eligible tribal members. Foley, a man who became more and more a friend to the Indian as his time in Congress progressed, did not yet perceive the Indian perspective on this particular issue. The Indian authors of both bills before the committee understood it completely, however, and knowingly used language that would weaken the position of tribal members dissenting via nonparticipation.

As various departments and offices within the government sent their positions on the bills to be included in the hearings record, so did the president's office. The office expressed concern: "We have no clear evidence that termination . . . is either necessary or desirable at the present time. So far as we know, the views of the tribal members have not been formally sought." The letter went on to acknowledge the assertion by the committee and the tribe that the majority of tribal members favored termination, but the president still suggested that the language of the bill be changed to reflect a decision made by a majority of eligible voters, not simply a majority of voters in the termination referendum. The letter further expressed the office's support of continued federal supervision: "We urge most careful consideration of the merit of termination, both from the Federal Government standpoint and that of the tribe."[12]

Narcisse Nicholson spoke first at the hearings in Spokane on November 3, and he carefully constructed his argument to depict termination opponents as having flawed characters and an irresponsible reliance on the government. Regarding unemployment statistics, Nicholson outlined industry opportunity on the reservation:

> There is no significant relationship between employment of Indians by industries on or near the reservation and Indian ownership of reservation assets. Evidence shows in the past Indians have not taken full advantage of job opportunities. . . . There has been [sic] over 800 jobs developed by the timber industry. . . . No more than 200 of those jobs are held by Colville Indians.[13]

Because of those statistics, Nicholson concluded, no effective argument could be made that termination would adversely affect Indian employment. Nicholson cited paternalism as the essential reason that some Indians could not be motivated to work or care for themselves. He outlined the various successes of Colvilles in ranching or other pursuits on the reservation, and indicated that because 70 percent of reservation tribal members owned their homes and managed their business, the majority of tribal members would not be harmed by termination of the communal status.

In response to the optimistic summary of the successfully engaged tribal members, Paschal Sherman raised a practical issue. He agreed with Nicholson that many tribal members employed on or near the reservation made enough money to live on without assistance, but Nicholson had neglected to include in his assessment the fact that, upon termination, the wages earned by those individuals or families would necessarily be allotted differently. Families could live on $3,000 a year because they had per capita payments from the tribe. Such payments averaged $150 per year, although the previous year tribal members had gotten two payments totaling $500. For a family of four, that represented an additional two thousand dollars. Furthermore, the end of federal supervision would mean the beginning of payment for medical services and property taxes, neither of which tribal members had

had to pay under the reservation system.[14] In other words, the addition of tribal dividends took Colville families closer to the 1965 US median income of $6,900, while tribal health and education benefits minimized expenses that would be out of pocket if the tribal entity did not exist.

Sherman also pointed out the flaws in trying to apply the Klamath model to the Colvilles. Roughly two thousand people had been enrolled as Klamaths, of which four hundred chose to remain. Consequently, the sale of Klamath resources provided enough money to pay the withdrawing members and still support the remaining members. Colville enrollment in 1965 totaled roughly five thousand. If a similar percentage chose to withdraw as had withdrawn from the Klamaths, almost all of the land and timber would have to be liquidated to support the withdrawing members. Little would be left to support the remaining members.

Norma Inks, of the Colville Indian Association, found herself agreeing with Sherman despite their being positioned on opposite sides of the issue. The Klamath experience was a cautionary tale, Inks advised, because of the fate of the remaining members, not the withdrawing members. She had visited several remaining members, as well as the bank trustee who managed their accounts, and had discovered great dissatisfaction among them. While the withdrawing members had taken their $43,000 payout, the remaining members left their shares as part of the corporation that managed their remaining lands and resources. The remaining members had recently been receiving only $1,600 a year in per capita payments from their tribal investments, which necessitated a withdrawal from their principal in order to pay for food and housing. When Inks spoke with one remaining member in the spring of 1965, she learned that their per capita payments had been reduced to only $800 a year. This remaining member asserted that many Klamaths believed that they could not live at the same standard as their withdrawing cousins could, and now wished that they had supported complete federal withdrawal.[15]

As Colville tribal members invoked the Klamaths throughout this hearing, other Washington and Oregon tribes testified about their concerns related to Colville termination. A contingent from the Yakama Reservation, located in south central Washington State, including tribal chairman Eagle Seelatsee and tribal council attorney James Hovis, also appeared before the committee to share their views. Seelatsee asserted that termination generally did not serve the best interests of Indians anywhere, but the Yakama had a more concrete concern: what would happen to the allotments on the Yakama Reservation that enrolled Colvilles had inheritance rights to or partial shares in? Tribal council attorney James Hovis told Colville tribal members that he had no intention of stepping into their business, but he did want to learn from the congressmen how the government would deal with Colville assets on Yakama land.[16] This issue exemplifies the reality that termination affected not only the tribe that experienced it but other tribes with whom they shared ties. The Colvilles had especially wide-reaching blood ties to other tribes because of the Entiat and Moses-Columbia bands' bonds in the Yakama region and because of numerous intermarriages between the Colvilles and the Spokane and Coeur d'Alene tribes.

Two representatives of the Warm Springs Tribe of north central Oregon voiced their concern related to Colville termination. Colvilles owned fewer than two hundred acres of Warm Springs land, but tribal chairman Olney Patt did not want to see that land go into open domain. He requested that the Warm Springs be allowed to purchase the shares the Colvilles owned, should termination proceed. Charles Jackson, a member of the Warm Springs legislative committee, said:

> I feel that one of these times that the Indians . . . might perhaps band
> together and talk these matters over as to what is in the future for our
> children and our grandchildren. We have a place now to live, a place
> that we call our own. . . . I don't believe that we should put this on a
> block and sell it back to the people who are taking care of our prob-
> lems. . . . We are neutral in this case, but like I said, the Indian people
> have a lot of things in common.[17]

The Spokane Tribe also submitted its opposition to the termination of the Colville Tribes, primarily because of land and allotment concerns. A member of the Nez Perce Tribe from Idaho objected to Colville termination as well, not just because of the land problems it would create but also because the Nez Perce would lose the reciprocal hunting and fishing rights they currently enjoyed with the Colvilles. Jesse Greene, a member of the Nez Perce Tribal Council, pointed out that several tribes in the area participated in these reciprocal arrangements, and that each tribe would suffer if one was terminated.[18]

The committee had not anticipated that the land questions or the reciprocity questions would emerge at the hearing, and it had no ready answer for the Yakama, Warm Springs, Spokane, or Nez Perce representatives. They promised to consult the BIA and the Department of the Interior to determine the best way to handle the questions they had raised. These issues, along with others affecting the larger Indian community, would remain important throughout the debate.

Several off-reservation tribal members testified in favor of termination. They wanted the freedom to plan their own destinies with a lump sum payment instead of having the tribe or the BIA portion out small per capita payments. Clotilda Black had worked hard all her life, but she could not get a pension because she owned an allotment. After having a stroke at the age of eighty-two, she sold her allotment and moved in with her daughter, Myrtle Ort. Black noted that she hoped the termination bill would pass so that she could live her last days with some of the creature comforts she had lacked so far. Her niece Betty Landreth also supported termination but indicated that even after it had occurred she would still be Indian. "I will not let them come and transfuse out my Indian blood, I am still proud of it."[19]

Violet Friedlander Abrahamson, who also lived off the reservation, was against termination and wondered why the tribal member who was so proud of her Indian blood stood ready to give it up. "Why does she want to take money for it? This is our heritage, this is not something they gave to us." Abrahamson made good use of her hunting and fishing rights and did not want to forfeit them in exchange for cash. She adamantly desired to retain both her status as an Indian and the rights attributed Indians by the government.[20]

After the Spokane hearings concluded, many tribal members returned to the reservation to attend the hearings in Nespelem. Narcisse Nicholson opened the hearings, expressing the position of the council and then his own opinion:

> It seems that termination for the Colville Tribes has stirred up the
> Indian political pressure groups all over the country. They look at this
> termination as some kind of a test course Congress is going to take.
> They really have their propaganda machines going. . . . They say that
> Indians on the Colville Reservation will have to move to the cities
> in large numbers and will all end up on welfare. The average person
> reading these exaggerated statements that appear in the newspapers

believes that the Indians are illiterate, living in hovels and dying of disease, and that their land base is their only hope.[21]

Nicholson had been so frustrated with outside groups' commentary on Colville termination that he had withdrawn the Colville Confederated Tribes from membership in all regional and national Indian organizations. In January 1965 the council passed resolutions, in votes of eight to five, to withdraw from the Affiliated Tribes of Northwest Indians and the Western Intertribal Coordinating Council.[22] In 1964 the council had declined an invitation from the National Congress of American Indians to attend their conference. The council had also formally requested that the Colville Tribes be removed from any legislative platform created by the NCAI, as well as from the membership roster.[23]

Joseph Garry, president of the NCAI from 1953 to 1959 and a leader in the Coeur d'Alene tribe, considered termination to be the policy that would "result in the end of our last holdings on this continent and destroy our dignity and distinction as the first inhabitants of this rich land." He worked closely with Frank George, Colville Tribal Council member and NCAI vice president, to fight Colville termination. He championed all Colvilles who opposed termination. The NCAI continued to vocally and actively oppose termination throughout the era by rallying both Indian and non-Indian groups.[24]

The tribal council was determined to manage the Colvilles' business without interference. It had created a small world for the tribe to inhabit, one that did not allow tribal members to benefit from exposure to any pan-Indian initiatives under way at the time. Because of the major victories won by the new pro-terminationist council members in the spring election, the council wanted to capitalize on every opportunity to remain in control and to remind critics that the tribal members had put them in place for that very reason.

Louis Camille, a Colville elder and member of the Lakes band, provided a poignant counterpoint to Nicholson's frequent statements about the fitness of the Colvilles to manage their own affairs:

> I am against this bill or any other bill for the simple reason that I am 74 years old. I don't have no education. . . . They are trying to jerk this land our from under us without [the government] fulfilling their duties. You just think for yourself, if you had a child 9 or 10 years old,

you open that door and you tell your little boy, "All right, you are on your own." Do you suppose that little boy is going to make it? That's what I put as an example, us people, just in grade school. If this here bill was to go through, we, us Indians, would be lost.[25]

Camille lambasted the council and the people who elected them for being greedy and shortsighted. The Indians had gotten plenty from their timber to date, but had spent it recklessly and thus had nothing. He feared that the same would happen with a termination payout. He continued:

There is no other man in this whole world has the privilege, the rights, that the Indians got. Why should I step down one step to be equal with the rest of the citizens of the United States? I am above. . . . I got a boy in the Army back there fighting somewheres now. I told him I am going to stand pat on trying to hold on to this land for you. You are out there fighting for your land and here while you are gone I am not going to sell it out from under you. I will do my damndest to try and save it for you.[26]

The subcommittee asked Camille if he ever thought he would want to step down to equality with non-Indians. No, he said, because Indians fared better with their privileges like hunting and fishing access than whites managed without them. Committee members continued to question him carefully about too much dependence on the government and the motivations of people living on the reservation, but Camille remained resolute in his opinions and gave the impression that he pitied the whites who lacked the skills and benefits that Indians possessed.

The elders were formidable at the hearings that day. Alfred B. Fry of Omak agreed so much with a comment made by Mary Catherine Louie, 113, in the Colville *Statesman-Examiner* that he quoted it to the subcommittee in refutation of BIA claims. Louis said, "I know what freedom was before the Indian Bureau. Well. Wards of the Government is a mild word for prisoners of war. I hope to live to see the day that I will be free once and for all."[27] Madeline Moses Covington Edwards, a descendant of Chief Moses and a member of several families that retain prominence on the reservation, spoke to the committee through an interpreter, her daughter-in-law:

As long as we live, we are going to hold on to this land. Our ancestors got the land for us and we want to keep it so. . . . We want to keep our land base. Not only to keep the land but also our custom. We don't want to let it die, too, we want all of that to be kept with the land. It used to be different, when we had a meeting and council of years ago, that meeting was held by Indians, but when you turn around you are facing mostly whites in your audience. The main purpose is to hold on to the land, not for ourselves, but for our future generations.[28]

George Friedlander, a Moses descendant and a cousin to council member Lucy Covington, testified that he did not support termination but could understand why others clamored for it. The council had been telling tribal members that they would receive $40,000 if they accepted termination, and that is why so many had spoken in favor of the legislation. When Senator Haley indicated that he did not know whether tribal members would get four dollars or forty thousand dollars, Friedlander proposed a solution, "You spent billions protecting Korea, Vietnam, why don't you appropriate some money, pay them [termination advocates] off, and leave us Indians alone?" This remark met with heavy applause.[29]

Several tribal members criticized the notion that the Colvilles could not take control of their own affairs, and they could not understand why tribal members did not support termination. Martha Johnson of Spokane observed, "Some of our people . . . say they are opposed to liquidation. Even these must know that we are, in fact, getting liquidation now. No one who sees those great trucks loaded with logs and lumber from our land can be blind to this truth." Her sister, Viola Anderson of Coulee Dam, focused on equality: "We have asked Congress to recognize the inequality of justice provided by separate legal status—Indians are the only legally segregated race in the United States—for no crime except that they are Indian."[30]

More than two hundred and fifty tribal members attended the meetings in Nespelem on November 4 and 5. According to one reporter, the meeting in the gymnasium was a gathering of "descendants of some of the great Indian chiefs—Moses, Kamiakin, and others—who also chase the elusive basketball."[31] One hundred and two tribal members put their name on the list to testify over the course of three days, although it rapidly became apparent that not everyone would be able to be heard. As a result, 227 tribal members submitted letters, almost 70 percent more people than had written in 1963. The continued efforts to raise awareness through tribal meetings and the *Tribal Tribune* increased individual participation in the termination debate. The recent hard-fought tribal elections also produced a great deal of interest in what would come next for the Colville Tribes.

The minority council members spoke first on the final day of testimony that November. Harvey Moses, Lucy Covington, Shirley Palmer, and Frank George opposed the termination of federal supervision:

> Non-Indians and tribal members of predominantly non-Indian blood quantum have a widespread misunderstanding and ignorance of what constitutes an Indian and his rights. On the subject of American Indians, most of our non-Indian citizens are imbued with the misconception that somewhere scattered around the West are Indian reservations and these reservations are something like concentration camps. . . . Many non-Indians, especially those in the East, have humanitarian instincts that say . . . the Indians should be free. . . . [These] people come up with proposals like that which emanated during the Eisenhower administration and which is now being revived by Senator Henry M. Jackson and Congressman Tom Foley to "free" the Indian.[32]

The minority members wanted to retain the land and benefits accorded the tribe when the reservation was created in 1872. They also resented statements suggesting that the Colvilles lacked the freedom of US citizenship because of the reservation. Indians had been granted full citizenship in 1924, and those who took allotments had gained citizenship at the time of their land tenure, many prior to the 1924 date. Just because the majority of tribal members proved competent to manage their own affairs, Moses and others reminded, the BIA still had a responsibility to fulfill.

The group acknowledged the division of opinions on termination and urged that far more research should be conducted before taking any action. They blamed the tribal members who followed "a mercenary trail to cash in" on tribal holdings and others who "do not want to make known that they may be of a small quantum of Indian blood, but they are most vocal when it comes to getting benefits as Indians."[33]

The four members of the minority on the council declared that the majority members were not acting in the best interests of the tribe but only sought self-aggrandizement and power. The majority group prevented the minority members from participating in any policy-making committees and did not observe the democratic ideals put forth in the Colville Tribal Constitution. In defiance of the majority council's position on other tribes or Indian organizations participating in the Colville termination discussion, Frank George introduced statements from the NCAI and the Affiliated Tribes of Northwest Indians.[34] The ATNI acknowledged the opposition of the majority council to hear their opinion, but said, "We look upon the terminationist viewpoint as something that conceals a basic deceit behind a façade of plausibility and pious platitudes."[35]

In addition to its general opposition to termination, the ATNI had similar fears of problematic land transactions stemming from terminated Colvilles' holdings on reservations throughout the country. Moreover, they worried that "fractionated blood members whose quantum of Indian blood is so low that their children are not entitled to be enrolled will be going to the polls participating in a referendum against the Indian parents who rely on the Federal trusteeship as a protection over their homeland and whose Indian children are the very nub of the need for continued tribal existence." In his personal statement, Frank George considered the differences in opinion between the full-blood Colville and the mixed-blood:

> We Indians of substantial quantum of Indian blood oppose enactment of S. 1413, H.R. 5925, and H.R. 6331. We who oppose termination do so with the guidance of learning and reason. We firmly believe that those expressing a desire for termination are doing so without alternative, finding fault but never favor, perceiving gloom on every side in being identified with Indianhood.[36]

Nancy Hall, a Lakes member from Okanogan, said she was proud of being a full-blood who had lived on the reservation most of her life, but she was also frustrated at the lack of community feeling among the bands on the reservation. "There are too many bands of Indians on this reservation, which causes bickering, greed, and jealousy. The people just can't get together." She worried that the tribal council had wasted money, which affected all of the Colvilles, and she felt that she and her family would be better off liquidating so they could invest the payout.[37]

When Shirley Palmer faced the committee to speak, she asked them where else in American life they could find instances of wards voting out their guardians. "This bill is unfair in giving the fraction blood members whose children are not on the rolls the right to vote away the rights of members whose children are enrolled members of the Tribe." The BIA should protect the Colvilles from this kind of injustice, she said. Palmer did not support termination in any fashion and believed that the BIA had a responsibility to support the Colvilles as long as any existed on the rolls. She also pointed out that the tribe would slowly dwindle as tribal members continued to intermarry, and that when the numbers got so depleted, the government could decide what it wanted to do.[38]

When Virginia Andrews, a Nez Perce, spoke out against termination, she observed that many practiced the old ways. Hunting and fishing held a deep cultural significance for the tribe, and she mentioned that her brothers and sons all participated in these activities as often as they could. She valued the rights Indians held in these pursuits and wondered how Congress would compensate tribal members for their loss. The subcommittee remained uncertain as to the method of compensation for hunting and fishing rights because the government could not tangibly acquire them as property or resources. The subcommittee doubted Congress would recognize the value of these rights in the same manner that the Indian perceived them.

Andrews took pride in being Indian, and she observed that her father, a tribal elder, also rejoiced in it: "He is proud of his heritage and [feels] that it is no biological disadvantage to be an Indian. Therefore, he believes that the Indian reservation is the last empire of the Indian race where the culture he stubbornly clings to is kept alive only at the tolerance of a culture alien to his own."[39]

A disenfranchised Colville Indian Association member addressed the committee to outline the reasons he favored termination, but also to blow the whistle on the organizational structure of the CIA. Robert Irwin had been the leader of the Oroville-Tonasket chapter of the CIA until the previous spring elections. When his chapter had tried to pay its dues and renew individual memberships, CIA executives would only renew them if they supported H.R. 6331. This new rule likely emerged in response to the Oroville-Tonasket chapter's passage of a resolution in favor of S. 1442 in the fall of 1964. At that time, Colleen Allen explained that the Oroville-Tonasket group had attended a CIA meeting in Seattle and had discovered that they disagreed with the executive committee. The Oroville-Tonasket chapter of the CIA supported S. 1442 because it protected all the tribal members—those who wanted to remain and those who wanted to withdraw.[40]

Irwin remained angry about the CIA's treatment of his chapter, but he expressed greater concern over the CIA officers' testimony that they spoke on behalf of seven hundred registered CIA members. When tribal members asked to see the CIA register, the association denied access. The CIA asserted their rights as a state organization, not a tribal one, and reminded tribal members that they did not have to share their membership lists. Individuals began asking if the list contained their names, and the CIA refused to answer even those questions. Finally, Irwin claimed, one of the CIA trustees admitted that their list contained the names of everyone who had ever been a member of the CIA, even inactive members, and also admitted to trying to list children on their registry rolls. No group could claim to represent a majority of the tribal members, Irwin continued, and the only way they would discover the membership's true feelings about termination would be through a tribal referendum, which the council should have held before creating any terminal legislation.[41]

Tempers shortened throughout the hearings, each side frustrated with the opinions of the others. Finally Geraldine Waggoner vented, "For God's sake, how long are you going to hold us Indians imbonded [sic] when our forefathers fought so long to be free. . . . Why don't you Senators do everything possible to get our termination bill through Congress so we can be fully citizens?"[42]

Lucy Covington was worried about the state of Colville readiness for termination. Education, sanitation, employment, and human resources on the reservation remained at substandard levels when compared to the majority of the US population. Tribal members still needed the BIA, she said, but not from a sense of entitlement on the Indian's part. "I don't believe that Indians are lazy," she said. "During WWII, Nespelem was deserted. Many were quickly trained and held jobs, and after the war those same people found themselves unemployed and back on their homeland, where they feel at ease." It was important for people to have a place to return to, for security, for restoration, for matters of heritage. "If anyone thinks that we are playing Indian, we are sorry to embarrass you, we don't play Indian, we are Indian, it isn't for anyone's amusement. We have been snickered at most of our lives and some of our tribal members feel this way, but they aren't ashamed to claim Indian blood just to receive benefits and ask for full shares."[43]

The drama of the debate lies within the ways that tribal members expressed themselves. Their imagery and their passion and their intelligence were clear. One tribal member who opposed termination, Caroline Orr, even submitted her opposition in poetic form:

We've been told that the time has come,
And, yet,
It needn't to have come at all,
For us to choose between our homeland
And a handful of paltry coin.
Some may look for "freedom";
Some may seek a "happier land."
My people,
It's here all about you
If you but understand.
History supports the claim,
Our forbears pointed the way,
We must not deny our heritage,
On this—
Or any other day.
Until forever can be measured,
Our role in life is cast.
We must honor our Indian heritage
And learn
From the pages of the past.[44]

CIA member Alyce Hallenius did not consider poetry at all in her assessment of the Colville Tribes, but instead spoke about the tactics of war. She had apparently changed her previous position about the importance of the land and her desire that the Colvilles should hold on to it, because she depicted the Petitioners Party as the supply line to and from the Bureau of Indian Affairs and queried, "If you are in battle, do you not find the supply line and disrupt it?" She wanted to "explode the myth that Chief Joseph was a Colville Indian" and told the committee that Joseph had had his own homeland and could have returned there. Instead he was "forced upon us when he and his people were brought here as prisoners of war and corralled in four square miles of land in the Nespelem Valley." Hallenius characterized the BIA as "playing footsie" with Joseph's band, which consequently allowed them to increase their power on the Colville Reservation, led by "the Modern Day Chief Joseph, Frank George." Because they were always a peaceable tribe, she continued, the Colvilles "do not venerate a blood-spilling warrior," and she lamented that George wanted "to pull the maneuver that his ancestor was famous for, a retreat that will mean the final extinction of his own people, as well as the Colvilles."

Grandchildren of Chief Moses spoke out against termination. Through a translator, Sadie Moses Wilson declared, "All of these people I listened to here call themselves Indian. I don't believe a word of it. I like to remain as an Indian. I am an Indian . . . and we are not proud of the white people." Margaret Piotote added, "We have a beautiful reservation. It is worth more than any money."[45]

The hearings closed without any resolution. No position emerged triumphant or even in the majority, and the CIA had suffered a serious setback. The approach to termination in each bill had been simplified from a two-step to a one-step process, but the issue itself had become no less complex. Tribal members remained dejectedly divided on this issue, and many manifested their objection to the other side's position in increasingly personal comments. The blood quantum question became pervasive in considering who deserved to choose and sometimes even to speak. Residency emerged as another key consideration, as did ancestry and the question of "belonging" to the tribe. Members of Chief Joseph's Nez Perce band weathered especially hard blows on that question.

While elders voiced their opinions, often through translators, young people remained conspicuously absent from the debate. It is not clear whether tribal members had to be of voting age—at that time, twenty-one years old—to participate or if young people just left the debate to the older generations. Many tribal members mentioned sons and brothers being in the military, active participants in the American experience, or in school, but few mentioned how these young people viewed termination. The debate continued on the reservation for seven more years, although it did not remain as important in Congress, which allowed some people to refine their arguments, some to disengage, and some to change sides.

HIGHWAY 21 SEVEN MILES NORTH OF KELLER

CHAPTER 5

"Come back from your pilgrimage to nowhere."

THE political heyday for Colville termination had passed by 1967. Although the Subcommittee on Indian Affairs would continue to engage with the Colvilles about termination, it was clear that they were responding to the Colvilles, not initiating the conversation. At this point, the subcommittee's consideration of termination was tied to the Colville restoration bill, not based in a strong belief in termination policy. And while Robert Bennett, the new commissioner of Indian Affairs and a member of the Oneida Tribe in Wisconsin, believed that Indians should live without federal supervision, he was among a dwindling few at the federal level who held this perspective. The hearings on the reservation in 1965 had drawn the largest crowd of tribal members in attendance at any of the Colville termination hearings, and had produced more letters and statements as well. They would also be the last subcommittee hearings held on the reservation. On June 8, 1967, the Subcommittee on Indian Affairs held hearings in Washington, DC, on S. 282, a bill that provided for single-step termination of the Colville Tribes and liquidation of assets, to be paid out to each tribal member. The bill called for a referendum to be passed by the majority of tribal members voting, then a survey of resources to determine the dollar value of each. The bill remained fundamentally similar to earlier bills, and government officials and tribal members posited many of the same objections that they had to earlier incarnations. Few supported passage of the referendum unless a majority of eligible tribal members voted in favor of it, and tribal members remained concerned that Congress was asking them to blindly accept termination without any concept of compensation. Tribal council member Harvey Moses indicated that in the present bill "the Indian doesn't know what he's voting for."[1]

The Office of the President reiterated its concerns about Colville termination—that it had not seen enough evidence of the Colvilles' readiness for termination or an indication that a majority of the membership supported it. The office disliked the voting language within the bill, as well as the requirement for complete termination. The president preferred S. 1413 from 1965, since it provided for payment of withdrawing members and also allowed those who did not wish to terminate to remain. The Colville authors of the bill had envisaged the government buying the forested lands of the reservation in the event that no one else would, but the president's office rejected this plan. The government already owned six million acres of commercial forest in Washington. The president's office offered its support for termination of the Colvilles only if the subcommittee amended the bill and included the president's suggestions.[2]

The Bureau of Indian Affairs had its own concerns about the bill. While a 1966 tribal opinion poll indicated that 73 percent of respondents supported termination, 30 percent of the surveys mailed had not been returned. At least a portion of tribal members who did not cast their vote had chosen to express their disagreement through silence. Robert Bennett visited the Colville Reservation for two days in March to try to understand what tribal members thought about termination. He also used the meeting as an opportunity to introduce tribal members to his own proposals. One of his options allowed tribal members to withdraw and liquidate or to remain and set up a federally chartered corporation, with the property held in trust and operated as a business. Another option would allow liquidation and withdrawal or continued residence on a reduced reservation that would remain under the reservation system.[3] Seventy-five percent of the land and timber would have to be liquidated to allow the reduced reservation to exist, and the reservation would be located in two separate areas: the Nespelem area and the Inchelium area.

The tribal council majority felt heartened to learn that Bennett and "key members of Congress" believed that the continued reelection of pro-termination candidates and the recent opinion poll was evidence of general Colville support for termination. Bennett indicated to the minority members of the council that they should choose what they wanted in a remaining reservation or corporation, because termination of the Colville Tribes seemed inevitable, and he himself favored it.[4] At a public meeting in Nespelem, attended by more than five hundred tribal members, Bennett explained his position and the position of the Interior Department: "They are not advocating . . . termination of any tribes, but whereas a tribe has taken a position that is what they want, then we feel that it is our responsibility to help them work out the best possible kind of terminal plan."[5]

Anticipating a varied range of responses to termination, Bennett encouraged tribal members to take positive action and reminded them that their time to create a plan had already been extended twice. The time had come to compromise, he suggested. Amid several confusing motions to amend S. 282—meaningless motions, since the meeting held no legislative authority—several poignant Colville voices emerged. Speaking through an interpreter, Madeline Moses and Sadie Moses Wilson, both elders and descendants of Chief Moses, indicated that they did not favor termination or compromise. They wanted to hold on to the land for their grandchildren and future generations. Lionel Orr, a recent high school graduate, warned the commissioner and others to be careful in their consideration of any proposal: "It [termination] will affect you, but it will affect young people like me more. Because we are the younger generation, and although we haven't got any voice or any say . . . it will affect your children and my children too, probably. . . . Examine things more carefully for your own children's sake."[6]

Moses George, of the elder generation, pointed to all of the intelligent tribal members in the room, on both sides of the termination argument, and asked tribal members why they persisted in fighting among themselves: "We get very emotional and point fingers at one another. . . . We've been that way since Columbus landed down there along the creek someplace. . . . [Now] we're left here with just a very few acres of Colville Reservation. . . . We've got to pull together."[7]

Throughout the meeting, various sides of the debate had invoked parliamentary procedure or *Robert's Rules of Order* to try to give the meeting some structure. Few reservation residents were acquainted with these practices, however, and the Colville Indian Association and the Colville Liquidation Promoters especially attempted to use them to dominate the meeting. Those groups kept introducing amendments to the bill, although at most they could only be taken as recommendations. Other tribal members simply ignored the rules and spoke as they pleased. Despite the intent to have motions on the table and seconds and calls to question, the meeting was still somewhat of a free-for-all.

Ultimately, the meeting provided no resolution, but Bennett had shared his opinions and indicated the direction the BIA expected Colville termination to go. During his testimony in Washington, DC, in June, Bennett had outlined his responses to S. 282, some of them born out of the March meeting. He opposed the voting language and said that the BIA would only support the bill if a majority of tribal members passed the termination referendum. Further, he proposed a seven-year withdrawal of federal supervision over those who chose to remain, instead of the four years that had been previously proposed. Bennett also proposed that co-owners of allotments be given first refusal rights in the event of a sale. If the allottees decided to sell the whole parcel, the tribe who controlled surrounding reservation land would be next in line to purchase. This would protect the land from going into open domain and non-Indian ownership. Indian leaders from various reservations in the Northwest agreed with Bennett's approach.[8]

At the conclusion of Bennett's testimony, a junior senator on the subcommittee, Mark Hatfield of Oregon, asked Bennett to describe the BIA's philosophy regarding termination and Indian affairs. In a display of bureaucratic finesse, Bennett tried to answer circuitously:

> The government has made commitments to the Indian people by treaties, acts of Congress, and so forth, and the government should carry out these commitments to the Indian people. When the government has carried out these commitments to the Indian people by way of their educational level, health level, and so forth, then I feel I have a responsibility to report this to Congress and that Congress . . . will then determine whether or not our services shall be withdrawn and terminated or whether for reasons that the Congress may decide they shall be continued. And in the past, the Congress has made several kinds of decisions based upon particular situations.

Senator Hatfield pressed him for a clearer answer, and still achieved only moderate success: "The basic philosophy is that Indian people as a group should have the right to own property in a common group; that as Indian people develop their ability to manage their affairs . . . [they] can ask the Secretary of the Interior to be able to take control over . . . the reservation."[9]

The conversation between the two men created a distinctive picture of the contemporary consideration of Indians. Hatfield held a deep concern that the government would push Indians aside too rapidly as it pursued Indians' self-sufficiency away from the federal system, and he regarded the government's responsibility to the Indian as a serious one. Bennett agreed that the government had responsibilities, but also asserted that all Indians and tribes would eventually need to become self-sufficient. Termination of relationships with the federal government played an integral role in that process.

Congressman Tom Foley observed that some people still thought in a shallow way about termination. While he acknowledged that tribal members who opposed termination had made many salient points about hunting and fishing rights and their desire for federal financial oversight, he still maintained that the Colvilles would succeed without federal supervision. He also asserted that opposition to termination had become quite popular among liberals, and he viewed this as one of the reasons why the trend to terminate tribes had slowed.[10]

The Oregonian, the paper of record in Oregon, had concluded that the termination experience of the Klamath Tribe was the reason for the suspension of termination zeal in Congress. Some Colville tribal members feared S. 282 would put them in a situation too similar to the Klamaths and that Colville termination would prove unworkable as well. Colville tribal members in Portland desired complete liquidation and freedom from the BIA. Marcel Arcasa, age eighty-four, said, "The great majority of Colvilles have become well-educated and valuable members of 'outside' life. They do not want to be treated as incompetent children anymore."[11]

Because the subcommittee held the hearings for S. 282 in Washington, DC, the tribal council voted to cover travel expenses for council members and for two members from each group on the reservation that had a position on termination: the Colville Indian Association, the Petitioners Party, the Colville Liquidation Promoters, the Oroville-Tonasket Group, and the Compromise Group. The Oroville-Tonasket Group had emerged in 1964 after splitting with the CIA. The Compromise Group had emerged since the hearings in 1965, and this marked their first appearance before the Subcommittee on Indian Affairs. This act of fairness from the tribal council may be surprising, given their adamant position on termination, but they clearly wanted the debate on termination to be a representative one.

The tribal council spoke first at the hearings, providing the committee with a brief outline of the events that had led them to the nation's capital that day. They used recent election results to emphasize the general membership's desire for termination—pro-termination council members remained in office or were reelected, thus maintaining a majority position on the council—as well as the results of an opinion poll mailed out the previous fall. The survey queried, "Do you favor termination and liquidation of the tribal owned reservation assets at fair value, with the proceeds distributed equally to the members of the tribes?" The council mailed 2,526 surveys to the membership and received 1,272 responses in favor, 491 in opposition, and 51 responses indicating no opinion. Sixty-two percent of returns from tribal members on the reservation and 82 percent of returns from off-reservation members favored termination.[12]

Narcisse Nicholson, chairman of the tribal council, reminded the subcommittee that each tribal member counted equally and that the council did not differentiate among members based on geographic presence or blood quantum. Issues of blood and geography had become increasingly sensitive as questions of "membership" and the distribution of assets moved to the forefront of the termination debate. Nicholson had written to the BIA to clarify that these issues had emerged out of political agitation and not from the council or even the majority of the membership. He also attempted to explain why these concerns held many in sway:

> History bears out the fact that, to the present day, they [Colvilles] have never become one homogenous group and, therefore, do not have the characteristics of a true tribe of Indians. This circumstance is largely explained by the early tendency of the Indians who were native to the area to assimilate themselves into the culture and society developed by a mixture of the races. While the Indians who were brought here from other areas have also adopted the ways of civilization, they have been less inclined to integrate by marriage with the white race. Thus, tribal enrollment of today shows that most members who are enrolled as Indians of full blood degree are descendants of the bands of displaced Indians. Regrettably, it is from the leaders of this group that we often hear and read suggestions that tribal rights should be conferred in pro-

portion to a member's degree of Indian blood. Members who are native to the area regard the suggestion of measuring tribal rights by blood degree as a direct unjustified attack on their prior rights of inheritance and is suggestive of penalizing them for the natural integration that has taken place.[13]

This lack of a unified "tribal" identity had been the original justification for the Colville Tribes' request for termination, and it remained a pervasive observation. The Colvilles' termination experience was different than that of other tribes involved in the issue, as Colville tribal members and factions continued to fight for termination years after the policy had fallen out of political fashion. By 1967, in consideration of Colville termination, many government offices and officials had no opinion on whether the tribe should be granted termination or not—a notable change from the initial stance of many officials in 1963. Many Colvilles cited the facts of their confederation: combined as people by executive order, they had voted against the IRA, enacted a constitution anyway, and experienced a persistent lack of consistent opinion among tribal members regarding termination. Even those members who had been on the same side of the issue could not come to agreement about the process for reaching their goal.

Thirty-five tribal members attended the hearings in Washington, DC, and nearly one hundred tribal members sent letters to be included in the record. This session would be the first to witness a softening of previously entrenched positions. The tribal council majority had for years advocated a complete withdrawal and payout, but they finally agreed that if Congress amended the bill to allow tribal members to remain on a reduced reservation, they would no longer oppose it. Other groups and many individuals who opposed termination also indicated that they would accept a termination bill if it allowed for a remaining population of tribal members.

Neighboring tribes, however, had not relaxed their vigorous opposition to termination. The Spokane, Coeur d'Alene, and Kalispel tribes sent their attorneys to the hearings, accompanied by a joint statement that they had prepared. Robert Dellwo, the longtime attorney for the Coeur d'Alene Tribe who had extensive experience in Indian affairs and issues, spoke for himself as well as on behalf of the tribes who had retained him.[14] In response to a question about whether the Indians who want termination should get it, Dellwo observed the complexities of the situation: "The fact that a single Indian is terminated may not have much impact upon a reservation . . . [it] has to be a discretionary thing, to be decided on the merits of that particular application, his position in his family, his personal readiness for termination. And in this discretionary consideration, his own wishes are just one factor, although it is an important factor."[15]

Dellwo further noted that referenda on these matters proved fallacious, because no referendum can express the needs and the differences of individual Indian people. He remained concerned that tribal members who were not prepared for termination would vote in favor of it right alongside those who had fully integrated into the non-Indian culture. It was not a matter of intellect but of experience, and he stated further that many of the Colvilles who currently favored termination would not be considered by the BIA as prepared to even own a fee title to their land.

The Spokane, Coeur d'Alene, and Kalispel tribes worried not just about the practicalities of land issues emerging after termination but also about the dangerous precedent the Colvilles would be setting. The tribes feared that the off-reservation Colvilles, if successful, would serve as an example for other tribes' members to seek similar financial satisfaction. They unequivocally rejected the concept of termination: "We abhor the principal of wholesale buy out, sell out, sudden liquidation type of termination earlier used for the Klamaths and now proposed for the Colvilles. It brings to naught a whole era of Indian history and development. Enacted, it becomes a confession of failure for both the Indians and the United States Government."[16]

This triad of Colville cousins called upon the Colvilles and the committee to recognize the greatness and potential of the Colville Indians and the reservation resources. They lamented the void that termination would leave:

No flag will rise on Colville termination day. There will be no salutes, no marching bands. The forests and lands will echo with the sounds of commerce and development, but they won't be Colville sounds. . . . We call on the Colvilles now, we their neighbors who see the smoldering spark of the once glowing embers of an ancient brotherhood slowly going out. Come back, Colvilles! Come back from your pilgrimage to nowhere.[17]

When Colville Tribal Council member Harvey Moses appeared before the subcommittee, his opposition to termination held echoes of the three tribes' entreaty. The government had a commitment to the Colvilles, and tribal members felt strongly because they belonged to a group recognized and valued by the government. "We want to retain the Indian rights and prerogatives that stem from legal and moral obligations of the national government," Moses said. He proposed that the Colvilles would fare better with the help of economic development plans and training than they would if set loose into the world without education.[18]

Conversely, the Colville Indian Association interpreted the government's responsibility to the tribe to mean "the early passage of just and equitable termination legislation for the Colville Indians." The CIA continued to bemoan the government's designation of Indians as separate people and noted that "it is simply not possible for any human being to benefit from an economy he does not control." Ronald Nelson, the new president of the CIA, railed against the BIA and considered it dictatorial and a form of bondage that the Colvilles needed to escape in order to be free citizens. He coldly observed that

> almost to an individual, the people expressing a desire to hold the reservation are the more elderly Indian people. In a matter of five or ten years these people will have passed from the picture. We are certain that the descendants of these people will have integrated into the society of this Nation and be dissatisfied with the administration of their reservation, as we are today, and be back here at your door for another termination act.[19]

The Colville Indian Association stood among the minority who refused to consider a compromise bill providing for part termination, part remainder. The Klamaths "dragged their feet for over a year," Nelson said, and the CIA did not wish to impose that kind of process upon their fellow Colvilles. Norma Inks, also of the CIA, told the committee that the CIA did not seek immediate liquidation of the reservation timber assets because that would prevent the Colvilles from getting a fair price. She urged the committee to demand a fair appraisal before disposing of the tribe's timber, and also asked that they not allow Congress to require a sustained-yield clause for the disposition. Inks understood that such a clause caused the Klamaths to lose $30,000 each from the original appraised value of their timber and that that mistake had resulted in the lawsuit the Klamaths had brought against the government. "We seriously question the Indian Bureau's motives as guardian of our interests," Inks said, "and therefore most respectfully request that the committee keep a watchful eye on their devious ways." She went on to say that the CIA strongly opposed a vote on termination before the appraisals had been completed, because "no responsible citizen would agree to sell his valuable property without first knowing what he will receive in return."[20]

The Petitioners Party, which always had been opposed to termination, appeared before the committee to communicate their recent surge in membership, largely comprised of young people who had recently attained the age of franchise. T. B. Charley reminded the subcommittee of the economic problems facing many tribal members and indicated that those circumstances had not changed. "We are, then, poor Indians in an area of poor people. We cannot imagine our going through termination regardless just so that we can be like these people in our class, just as poor and even poorer." He called upon the subcommittee to "leave the Colville Reservation as it is for humanitarian reasons, in recognition of abiding rights, and in the interest of sound government."[21]

Paschal Sherman told the subcommittee that the Petitioners Party would not support a compromise bill for a remaining group on a reduced reservation because the smaller reservation would not be economically sufficient. Sherman's opposition was based on a conclusion that off-reservation tribal members would withdraw and extract payment, necessitating the sale of timber and forest lands, which would consequently cause those remaining on the reservation hardship and dependence on the lower incomes from grazing and mineral rights. Barbara Nicholson wondered why Congress had not learned from the lessons of the Klamath and Menominee terminations. She reminded the subcommittee of the burden placed on the respective states once federal supervision ended, and noted that the state of Washington and Ferry and Okanogan counties could not anticipate how much tribal members would need:

> I cannot see where the Congress, in its better judgment, could possibly pass another termination legislation for the Indians. . . . There has [sic] been so many repercussions and after effects which are not beneficial to the Indian people of our nation that proves that termination for an

Indian tribe is not the answer. We do not want our Colville people to experience such a tragic step at this time.[22]

Robert Irwin, a member of the Oroville-Tonasket Group, was impatient with his peers. Those tribal members who pled with the committee to save the reservation for their children, he charged, were out of touch with the reality of the twentieth century. Irwin worried that the Indian youth would suffer from a lack of integration into the non-Indian culture if they always had the reservation as a fail-safe. He endorsed careers in science and engineering and indicated that education would be even more important than the old ways: There is nothing about reservation life that prepares a boy to take a man's place in today's world. . . . Indian children will either be trained to live in today's world or they'll end up like museum pieces, or like buffalo in the park. There isn't much future for a child if he is kept segregated so palefaces can drive through a reservation to show their children what a real, live Indian looks like."[23]

Hank Adams, chairman of the Washington State project of the National Indian Youth Council (NIYC), spoke in response to Irwin's comments.[24] The NIYC opposed termination and felt that insufficient consideration had been given to the long-range effects of termination on all age groups, but especially the youth. The loss of the reservation could not be quantified for any of the residents. Adams considered the state of Washington unprepared to support the increased needs of the Colville Indians should termination proceed. He anticipated that state services would witness a rise in requests without a budget to support them, which would adversely affect all residents dependent upon those services.

Adams also declared the subcommittee out of touch with the national political mood: "The Senate Committee has not demonstrated itself to be responsive to the positive programs and policy changes of the Kennedy and Johnson administrations—and now appear inclined to repudiate them outright."[25] Adams felt that the committee failed to respond to or observe new interpretations of Indian policy, and favored the old approach to policy that did not include any advance input from tribal communities. The NIYC used the Colvilles as an example of the larger Indian experience and a cautionary tale for termination:

The effect of termination . . . is to remove the Indian from being the most closely-associated citizen to the federal government toward being the citizen most remote from it. . . . We are appalled that—as American Indians enter our fifth decade as United States citizens—our citizenship should be misused as preface, pretext, and total justification for all perverse policies.[26]

The Affiliated Tribes of Northwest Indians, founded in 1953 specifically to oppose termination, observed, "Those living outside the reservation boundaries should not be permitted to impose their will upon the actual residents of the reservation." Executive director Angela Butterfield further reminded the committee that president Dwight D. Eisenhower had provided for termination only with the consent of Indians, and since not all Colvilles supported termination, the Affiliated Tribes of Northwest Indians wanted to be on record opposing Colville termination.[27] Vine Deloria Jr., executive director of the National Congress of American Indians, feared that the BIA influenced the Colvilles' desire for termination: "We believe that the Colville people are stampeding toward something they don't understand."[28]

Virginia Andrews, who had traveled from the reservation, said she felt "at the mercy of the so-called 'majority' whose sole interest in termination springs from the projected sale of tribal forest lands." What would they do without federal health services, even if tribal members got to keep a small portion of the reservation? "The clinic at the old agency hospital site has many tribal members calling for medical assistance and the clinic calls will total well over 7,000 this fiscal year."[29] Health services affected many tribal members, but especially children and the elderly. Because few reservation residents held year-round employment, few tribal members had health insurance. They depended on these services for everything from cold medicine and vitamins for babies to sports physicals for school children to contract care for serious medical procedures. In 1965 federal and tribal expenditures for social services on the Colville Reservation exceeded $570,000.[30] Termination would leave a gaping hole for people who counted on this support close to home. While off-reservation tribal members would say that they received none of these benefits, it had been their choice to leave the reservation and forfeit the free care. Furthermore, should any off-reservation tribal members wish to return and reside on the reservation again, they would be able to enjoy all of the services at that time.

The essential question of fairness emerged throughout the termination debate. Which group had a stronger "right" for their side to be championed by the government? Reservation residents reminded off-reservation members that they had chosen to leave. Those who lived in cities responded angrily that the reservation had no future to offer them, no educational opportunities, no chance for career growth, and no modern conveniences. They condemned reservation residents for living in a romanticized past with no eye on the future. Victor Campobaso said:

> I can't see why the big majority of Colville Tribal Indians who are in strong favor of termination settlement have to have our rights or justice be in jeopardy on account of these Colville Indian members who oppose termination. I don't see where these Colville tribal members who oppose termination and the Bureau of Indian Affairs do the entire Colville Indians any good.[31]

The issue of collective rights versus individual rights loomed large for the Colvilles during the 1960s. Reservations have been considered socialistic or communistic entities because of their collective nature.[32] The Colvilles would not describe themselves as either socialists or communists, but group identity existed whether the bands valued intragroup or intergroup relationships.

This question of identity, along with the question of whose rights should be considered more representative, framed the termination debate. Tribal members on the reservation largely identified with their own bands. Many off-reservation members did not identify with their reservation cousins, a behavior based on fear of the racial prejudice that pervaded the 1950s. That decade left many Indians feeling ashamed of their heritage; they faced discrimination alongside African Americans, and consequently many Indians denied their blood. Many Colville tribal members report that their grandparents and parents often refused to speak the Colville dialects with them as children because they wanted the children to learn to "talk white" in order to succeed in the white world.

Of course, innumerable tribal members valued the reservation as their home and as part of their heritage. Adriana Lee Fry, a lifelong Inchelium resident and member of the Lakes band, appealed to the committee, "I am against termination. There aren't very many reservations left in this country and I think we should keep ours because we are a vanishing race as it is." Many tribal members spoke and wrote to the subcommittee that they wanted to protect and preserve the reservation for their enrolled children. Clarence Hoffman explained, "I have six boys and I want them to be raised on the reservation and benefit from it as I have."[33]

The first high school student on record in the debate was sixteen-year-old Theresa Vallee, a student at the Riverside Indian School, who spoke for herself, in opposition to her mother, about the battle dividing her reservation:

> If termination is inevitable, then I shall try to accept it, but my heart
> shall not be in it. What use will it be to have the color of an Indian,
> if you cannot claim right to any certain denomination of the Indian
> nation as whole? When we, as a tribe, terminate, we give up that right.
> It is a right that no other nationality can proudly claim. Thus I am sorry
> to see such a glorious heritage pass out of existence.[34]

Emily Peone, from the Lakes band, wanted to retain the reservation in order to "remind our children that they are part of a once-great and proud race of people." She went on to say that the young people should have a voice in this debate, because they would be most harshly affected by termination.[35] Sarah Finley agreed with tribal members who wanted to protect the land for the generations to come, and she also included a history lesson:

> You are not supposed to force any law on us without our consent. . . .
> You say this is a country for all—justice, freedom and the pursuit of
> happiness. I am waiting to enjoy these freedoms. I am 85 years old—
> had eighteen children—and worked like a slave without any help from
> the Bureau. . . . I think it is a disgrace. This is the last piece of what is
> truly our homeland. We are going to keep it. No law or anything is going
> to cheat us out of it. . . . May God forgive me for what I wrote, but it is
> true. I have been under the Bureau and I know what it is like.[36]

Kathleen Burke's letter to the subcommittee was tinged with sadness. She had observed the behavior of tribal members at the termination meetings with a deep regret, as many mocked the traditional ways that others valued. She did not like the aspersions cast because some Indians chose not to marry outside the tribe. "Is it so wrong to want to stay a full blood Indian?" She felt remorse at the treatment of the bands added to the Colville reserve: "The late Chief Jim James adopted them into our tribes and called them brothers. It wasn't their choice to be displaced."[37]

Charley Williams, an elder, dictated a letter to be sent to the committee:

> We who live on the reservation want our side given careful consideration and not give full credence to those absentee tribal members who want to sell our tribal estate right out from under us. . . . I belong to a much older generation of Indians and like most of them I have a close attachment to the land base. It is an important part of our way of life and our views deserve the respect of the Congress of the United States.[38]

Williams's statement brought forth an important idea—respect. Congress had supported termination for the Colvilles because some Colvilles claimed the majority favored the policy, and some congressmen would claim that they had proceeded out of respect for the Colvilles and their wishes. It is not apparent, however, that members of the subcommittee allowed themselves to be well enough acquainted with the tribal members to know whether their own actions would be viewed as respectful or disrespectful.

Certainly within the tribal debate, many individuals ignored the importance that respect played as a rule of behavior, especially its importance in traditional ways. A tribal member had indicated that silence expressed disapproval. That particular cultural tradition can be found among other indigenous populations.[39] Likewise, the fact that many elders chose to speak in their native dialect instead of English also held a lesson for the subcommittee and the audience: in effect, being Colville still matters and I am reminding you of that.

A changing mood emerged during these hearings in 1967, one of weariness. The tribal council's acquiescence to compromise indicated its desire to proceed with termination, even if the plan did not include all of the council's designs. Commissioner Bennett's suggestion for compromise illustrates the BIA's desire to reach closure on the issue. By this time, the BIA had been working with the Colvilles for eleven years to craft an agreement on termination. Bennett tried to take a firm hand with the Colvilles, and intimated that if they did not choose a path toward termination, then he would. Only the subcommittee could move the bill toward approval, however, and it retained an earnest desire to learn whether most Colvilles really did favor termination.

Active membership in tribal termination groups on both sides of the question had waned by 1967. The apex for tribal members' involvement in the debate was 1965, when it was clear that tribal members from both off and on the reservation wanted their opinions heard and counted. In subsequent years, however, tribal members realized that the debate had not advanced since the council submitted the initial termination bill in 1961. Many members lost interest in continuing to assert their opinions on the matter when the debates never resulted in action. Furthermore, tribal members remained protected from the imposition of termination because any bill would require approval through a tribal referendum.

The year 1967 witnessed more vocal opposition from other Indian groups. As the effects of Klamath and Menominee termination became more widely known, tribes in the Colville locality as well as pan-Indian organizations appealed to the subcommittee to refuse Colville termination. These groups feared that the Colvilles had underestimated the effects that termination would have on them. Tribal members who believed that a cash settlement was a solution to loss of heritage and rights angered external Indian groups. Their larger concern remained the retention of Indian rights. National Indian organizations considered pro-terminationists indifferent to the experience of the national Indian community, an opinion reinforced by the council's complete withdrawal from Indian organizations outside the Colville Reservation.

The Tribal Business Council remained steadfastly committed to ending federal supervision over the Colvilles. Termination proponents had held on to their majority position on the council and consequently considered the council body representative of tribal members' needs. The council agreed to compromise only if necessary, and many council members expressed opposition to this idea.

By 1967 the Senate had approved two Colville termination bills, but both died in the House. S. 282 would meet the same fate. It passed in the Senate in August 1967 but was reintroduced in 1968, with a companion bill in the House. The political shift against termination would be even more evident by that time, and the 1968 hearings, the final hearings on Colville termination, would also be held in Washington, DC. The subcommittee did not venture to the reservation to hear testimony for and against Colville termination, which gave a nonverbal indication that the issue had been downgraded in importance. Many tribal members refused to give up, however, and participated in the debate to the fullest extent of their ability. In 1968 tribal members would have their final opportunity to share their opinions on termination and engage with the congressional subcommittee.

GRAND COULEE DAM

CHAPTER 6

"Not another inch, not another drop."

IN July 1968, in a last-minute hearing jammed into an empty morning slot of the full congressional session calendar, the Subcommittee on Indian Affairs met one more time to listen to Colville tribal
members. It had been a year since the subcommittee had heard arguments for and against Senate Bill 282. That bill had not advanced, so
had been reintroduced alongside a companion bill, House Resolution
3051.

When Tom Foley had introduced H.R. 3051 in 1967, he had said that
the "Colville Confederated Tribes have shown both their desire for termination of federal supervision and their capacity and readiness for
termination."[1] This hearing would differ considerably from past meetings. Because the committee had to find space on the legislative calendar on short notice, tribal members did not receive enough notification
for many to plan to attend. Only council-sponsored individuals testified in person—council members and two representatives from each
of the various parties involved in the termination debate. A few tribal
members sent statements to be read at the meeting, but, for the most
part, the representatives spoke for themselves and their respective
groups. Because the subcommittee voted on H.R. 3051 at the end of the
meeting, they did not accept letters or statements after these hearings.

The subcommittee had a few new members, which altered the
momentum of the hearing. New subcommittee members did not have
the same familiarity with Colville termination as their peers enjoyed.

One committee member, Congressman John Saylor of Pennsylvania, demonstrated his inexperience with Indian culture when he asked each tribal member about their enrollment status and degree of Indian blood. Several tribal members became defensive when they admitted to having only one-eighth or one-sixteenth Colville blood. Congressman Saylor seemed not to comprehend the implication behind his question, that blood degree should be a factor in the debate.

Congressman Thomas Pelly, of Washington State, submitted a statement withdrawing from consideration the bill he had submitted on behalf of the Colville Indian Association. The CIA considered their new bill similar enough in intent and language to S. 282 to meet its termination goals. "The Colville Indian Association and those in accord with its views are in complete harmony with the Congress and its desire to completely terminate Federal supervision over the Colville Indians."[2] Pelly asked only that the committee amend the CIA bill to remove the right of the secretary of the Interior to determine the fair market value of the timber in favor of three independent appraisals.

Narcisse Nicholson, chairman of the tribal council, offered the first testimony on behalf of the Colvilles. Termination had been an issue for so long, he said, because tribal members had little reason to plan for a common destiny. Forced occupancy as a tribe "did not create a common bond but only intensified the rivalry and long held bitterness built up over time between the bands who occupied separate parts of the territory." These fractured relationships had enjoyed ample time for healing, but Nicholson concluded that a true sense of brotherhood would never emerge. In requesting termination, "We are asking the Congress to enact legislation which is the result of recognition that the clock cannot be turned backwards. . . . We cannot pretend that true tribalism exists on the Colville reservation." Nicholson felt it would be corrupt to try to retain a tribal entity where none existed.[3]

Nicholson went on to say that communal ownership had done a disservice to those who worked hardest, because in a communal environment, the needs of the greater community must be considered before individual needs. He believed that this proved a disincentive for self-improvement and "caused serious inequities to the Indian [land] owners." Nicholson reminded the subcommittee that a dominant Colville culture did not exist and that "semblances of heritage occur only in isolated instances." Consequently, with the needs of the majority in mind, the council respectfully requested that the tribe be terminated so that the Colville people could exercise individual freedoms: "We have no desire to be swept up in a tide of anti-termination policy of Indian groups who hold differing views. Each tribe should be judged on its individual merits and circumstances."[4] This was a reminder to the subcommittee to value the word of the Colvilles over that of the initiatives of national Indian groups or even Native communities adjacent to the Colville Reservation.

The council also proposed that the Department of Agriculture appropriate money from Congress in order to purchase tribal forests in the event that a satisfactory market price could not be found.[5] The council considered that a federal purchase of these resources was the only way to ensure a fair price and proper procedure. This requirement remained one reason the bills never passed in the House. The subcommittee members continued to doubt that Congress would allocate money for this kind of purchase. Representative James Haley, the chairperson, remained especially skeptical. When the Bureau of Indian Affairs retained the Stanford Research Institute to assess the value of human and natural resources on the Colville Reservation, the SRI had valued the timber at a minimum of one hundred million dollars, and the Okanogan County forester estimated that it could be worth as much as one quarter of a billion dollars. Haley knew that the congressional budget did not have reserves of that kind in any line, and he also understood that the Colville situation would not be considered critical enough for any congressional allocation.[6]

Two other council members asserted their desire for termination in order to be free of the Bureau of Indian Affairs. Roy Seyler and Alice Lawrence told the committee that they had lived on the reservation all their lives and that their friends and neighbors thought and behaved the same as did any citizen of the United States. These tribal members wanted to remove their assets from the control of what they believed were corrupt US government officials who had mismanaged the Colvilles' affairs: "Our people do want to gamble with what they left." Many tribal members felt comfortable with their property and their finances and would rather try to do manage them on their own than depend on the Bureau. "We don't know of any time that the Indian Bureau ever bought groceries for anyone in our district. . . . The people have always had to shift for themselves." Council members Seyler and

Lawrence believed that all Colvilles would be better off away from the BIA and with the freedom to plan for their own futures.[7]

Lucy Covington spoke on behalf of the minority members of the council. The voting method remained one of her primary concerns with the bill. It was disconcerting to her that young people and children could not vote in the termination referendum, because they comprised nearly half of the reservation membership. The reservation belonged to them, too, and they should have equal participation rights.

Covington also believed that termination seemed premature. Throughout the termination debate, she said, nothing had been done to develop tribal resources because no one knew when termination would be enacted. Consequently, management of the Colville Reservation had been stagnant for nearly fifteen years. Covington pointed out the new government programs designed to educate tribes on economic planning and resource development and said that it would be a shame to end federal supervision before utilizing these programs to the fullest extent. She also told the committee that the tribe had been making great strides toward higher education for tribal members. The tribe and the government had allocated more money for education, and many tribal members embraced the opportunity to go to school. Covington considered it a waste to let those improvements result in nothing when they forecast a brighter future.[8]

In consideration of the payout option, Covington concluded, "Liquidation means only one thing, as I said, that would be that they want money. Money will not solve the Colville problem or the Indian problem." She believed that the advocates of liquidation had a simplified conception of the payment process: they thought that tribal members would vote, then a short time later get a check from the government. Covington knew that it would not be that simple and that a lengthy process of valuation and disposition lay ahead if termination progressed. Many tribal members would be angry about the months without payment and they would wish to reverse their vote. "Then what? You can't turn the clock back," she warned. Covington feared, as did her peers in the minority, that the Colville people still did not fully comprehend the implications of termination, despite every effort to delineate it clearly. Ultimately, she worried, people would say that they had not been informed, but by that time, it would be too late.[9]

Finally, Covington addressed asset allocation. She believed, and had always asserted, that cash distribution should be based on blood quantum. "Since I am not a full-blooded Indian . . . I don't feel I should be getting 100 percent. . . . I should get 75 cents out of every dollar that others would get." Covington felt that a payout based on percentage blood quantum would prove the most equitable and would include everyone on the rolls, even those with one-eighth or one-sixteenth blood.[10] While the committee did not comment on Covington's suggestion, Haley must have been envisioning an accounting quagmire if they chose to accept that proposal.

Alice Huber, president of the Colville Liquidation Promoters, also addressed the issue of blood. "I feel very strong that all our Indians deserve equal respect for their intelligence," she said, "and that it is morally wrong for anyone to try and judge the Indians by their color or degree of Indian blood." She was angry at those tribal members who intimated that the full-bloods possessed a weaker intellect that those tribal members of mixed heritage. "It detracts from their dignity for others to claim superiority and the right to rule their lives for them."[11] The Colville Liquidation Promoters had an important mission, she said, that the Colville people agreed with. In annual elections, CLP candidates had built a ten-to-four majority on the tribal council, and had retained it for five years. Huber concluded that if the Colville people did not truly desire termination, then they would not have kept electing pro-termination candidates.

The 1968 tribal council election created conflict. The votes from the four district polling places produced a loss for the CLP that year, but once the election committee tallied absentee ballots, the CLP candidates emerged victorious. Candidates ran their campaigns on one issue—termination. Consequently, the council elections can be understood to represent pro-termination votes and anti-termination votes. The absentee voters favored termination in a ratio exceeding two-to-one.[12] Reservation tribal members regarded the results as an inequity because many believed their votes should count more than the votes of off-reservation tribal members. Furthermore, the CLP refused to acknowledge the split in votes and accused minority members of the council of playing politics in an effort to turn the people against them.

An old argument surfaced when Congressman Haley asked Lucy Covington if the CLP candidates who won the council majority had promised tribal members a specific dollar amount when the tribe's assets were liquidated. Covington said that CLP members had suggested specific cash values if termination occurred, but Huber vehemently denied that CLP members ever assigned dollar amounts to the proposed termination: "We have not and do not intend to even begin to estimate the value of a tribal member's interest in the tribal holdings if Congress should authorize a division of the assets. We feel strongly that, aside from the money involved, there are principles involved because the federal government is not recognizing that the tribal era has passed."[13]

T. B. Charley of the Petitioners Party argued against Huber's claim that the tribal era had passed, and used his testimony to produce several examples of a strong tribal base. He had statistics to illustrate that the Colvilles still needed the reservation structure as well as their tribal identity. The 1968 Citizens Board of Inquiry into Hunger and Malnutrition in the United States included the Colville Reservation in their geographic distribution of hunger within the United States. Charley asserted, however, that starvation did not exist on the reservation. "Within the reservation community, Indians help one another as they have done in centuries past. This points to what may be expected if the reservation community, with its traditional ties of mutual assistance, should be broken up by termination."[14] Charley felt that the importance of cooperation among reservation members should not be underestimated. While Nicholson had claimed that instances of heritage endured among only a few tribal members, Charley proposed that many individuals observed traditional Colville values—such as sharing with the community—on a regular basis. Young people often assisted elders with heavy chores, such as wood retrieval and stacking, and brought deer for the winter. The family structure still included interdependence among generations, and children learned a great deal from their elders.

Charley also reminded the committee of President Lyndon Johnson's message to Congress in March, when he had proposed a new goal of development for the American Indian, "a goal that ends the old debate about termination."[15] Johnson clearly intended for Indians to participate in his Great Society. Charley concluded that the Colvilles would be better off following the president's new vision for the Indian and developing the reservation resources. He suggested that the tribe could benefit greatly from developing the tourist trade as well as some orchard sites, and estimated that the income generated by the success of these endeavors would please even those who wanted to liquidate. Tribal members would be glad they had not chosen to terminate.[16]

Barbara Nicholson of the Petitioners Party provided a 1967 resolution by the National Congress of American Indians (NCAI) opposing Colville termination. Nicholson observed that the Colville Business Council did not hold memberships in any national Indian organizations "due to the conflictions [sic] of philosophies and/or policies engendered or fostered by them." Despite the Colvilles' status as nonmembers, several members of the Petitioners Party attended the NCAI conference as observers and held memberships in the organization.[17]

The NCAI remained interested in Colville termination because of the far-reaching effects it could have on the national Indian community, and the organization adopted a resolution against Colville termination. The resolution observed that the majority of Colville members who favored termination resided off the reservation and possessed only a small degree of Indian blood and also that tribal members who opposed termination had property and cultural interests on the reservation. The NCAI believed that Colville attainment of termination would have ill effects on other tribes because the Colville situation would serve as an example for other urban Indians who had no interest in returning to the reservation and instead hoped to exchange their tribal membership and tribal rights for cash.[18]

Members of the NCAI also worried about how Colville termination would affect indirect parties. The NCAI cited the Coeur d'Alene Tribe as an example. Membership in the tribe required one quarter Indian blood, not Coeur d'Alene blood. Thus Coeur d'Alene tribal members who got a portion of their blood from Colville heritage could be cut from their own rolls in the event of Colville termination. Although these Indians possessed Colville blood, they had no vote in Colville business because they were not enrolled members at Colville. Four hundred and sixty-four members of other tribes reportedly held property interests on the Colville Reservation, and the NCAI feared that their rights would be unprotected in the Colville termination process.[19] Citing the Klamath and Menominee experiences, the NCAI worried that the state and counties remained unprepared for the consequences of termination:

The states and counties also discover that the social and cultural stability of the tribal members tend to disappear when their tribal identity is lost. The result is retrogression, a disappearance of tribal standards, their traditions and joint discipline which sustained the tribal Indian members as law-abiding, contributing citizens. The breakdown, the disappearance of the tribe is analogous to the break-down and disappearance of family groups, long recognized as the warp and woof of social and moral stability.[20]

Congressman Tunney had familiarized himself with tribal member perspectives on termination, and he asked Paschal Sherman if he and the Petitioners Party opposed the compromise solution offered in S. 282. Sherman asserted that the reduced nature of the reservation would lead to reduced resources, and he indicated that some members believed that any form of compromise would allow the pro-terminationists to achieve victory. Sherman outlined the eventualities of termination, as he perceived them: most members would take the cash payment and force those who remained to live on greatly reduced land-holdings. Sherman estimated that after the timber and land resources had been liquidated, the smaller reservation would be able to support only approximately one hundred individuals. Tunney pressed the point and wondered if Sherman simply did not want the majority members of the tribe to have their say: "Apparently you are opposed to this bill because you feel that if the people had a free choice they would opt for the money rather than for remaining on the reservation as an integral tribal unit. You feel that this is undesirable that they have this free choice?"[21]

Sherman countered Tunney's conclusion. He promoted free will among all people, he said, and simply endeavored to make the subcommittee, especially the new members, understand what the remaining members would face on a post-termination Colville Reservation.[22] He also introduced a previously unconsidered nuance into the discussion. Few of the pro-termination members had strong feelings about the actual end of the Colvilles as a tribal entity, he said. The majority of the urban pro-terminationists wanted cash and favored the removal of Federal supervision because it would result in liquidation. If they could have liquidation and retain a cultural designation as Colvilles, then few would oppose that opportunity. This interpretation of the debate indicated that, for the most part, tribal members did not reject Indian identity. They simply wanted to cash in on reservation resources before the BIA mismanaged them out of existence or before individual Colville blood diluted to the point of being off the rolls.[23]

Congressman Haley interjected at this point to review some information about the two leading termination examples, the Klamath and the Menominee. Some Klamaths had indeed run through their settlement with nothing to show for it, he said, but the government could do little about it. The Menominee had lost significant land and industry as a result of their termination process. "Just last session we had to supply additional funds because these people were really in want. . . . The Appropriations Committee [provided] a substantial amount of money for them. I think we have to keep that up." Haley questioned whether the state of Washington would be prepared to assist the Colvilles after termination, or if Congress would have to step in to help.[24]

Sherman doubted that the state and counties fully comprehended what the end of federal supervision over the Colvilles would mean for them. Sherman indicated that the state would not necessarily have a bigger tax base upon termination, because the sale of land and resources would be tax-free. The Colvilles would also enjoy forbearance of property tax as part of the proposed termination settlement. Consequently, unless the Indians sold considerable amounts of their own land to taxpayers, the state and counties would absorb a land base and have to maintain the roads, sanitary facilities, and so forth without gaining the tax base to go along with it.[25]

Many tribal members who opposed termination, as well as pan-Indian groups and congressmen, had grave concerns over the readiness of the state to accept members of a dissolved Colville Tribe. The state had not participated in the debates, perhaps because it considered termination a federal issue. State officials' testimonies regarding the breadth of the states' resources would have given federal lawmakers a more complete picture as they attempted to draft legislation. Ferry and Okanogan counties had both asserted their preparedness for the event, and they felt their financial estimates to be accurate because they had absorbed some aspects of law and order from the tribe under Public Law 280. However, the tribe also paid each county forty thousand dollars per year for these services, income the counties would lose if the tribe terminated. As the weaknesses of the Klamath and Menominee termination processes became more apparent every day, evidence that the state of Washington would not suffer as a result of Colville termination would be crucial to advancing any termination bill.[26]

Chair of the Oroville-Tonasket Group Robert Irwin grew impatient with the discussion of Washington State and brought the subcommittee's focus back to the concrete matter of Indian well-being. He favored complete termination because he perceived it to be the route to Indian progress:

> I hear it said that members of my race should follow the Indian path to the white man's way. But there is no Indian path leading into the American mainstream. The Indian path leads the other way. . . . If Indians are ever going to learn to live like white people, in the white man's economy, they are going to have to live with the white people. . . . The Indian Bureau and the professional Indians talk so much about preserving the Indian land base that it sounds as if land is more important to them than people. In my opinion it's time to stop worrying about what's happening to Indian land and give more attention to what's happening to Indian children.[27]

In addition to his concern that the Indian Bureau attempted to retain control over the Colvilles by dragging their feet about termination, Irwin also resented interference from other tribes and Indian organizations. Other groups should have no input on Colville termination, he said, because Colvilles answered only to themselves. Irwin urged the Subcommittee to disregard any testimony from nontribal members. Ronald Nelson, president of the Colville Indian Association, echoed Irwin in his appraisal of the BIA's reluctance to relinquish control over Colville affairs. Nelson believed that termination provided the only option for advancement and progress. Individuals needed to be in charge of their own affairs in order to create personal initiative. As long as tribal members could rely on a collective to care for them, Nelson concluded, many would continue to fail and be willing victims of paternalism. "The bureau and those who benefit have no right to hold the Indian people in economic bondage."[28]

Nelson also desired several amendments to S. 282 and H.R. 3051 on behalf of the CIA. While Pelley had withdrawn the proposed CIA bill at the beginning of the hearing and indicated that the CIA supported S. 282, Nelson made it clear that his organization offered limited support of S. 282 and the companion bill as currently written. He wanted the appraisals of tribal land and resources completed prior to the tribal referendum on termination so that tribal members would know the dollar value of the termination package before making a decision on their position. In addition, Nelson opposed the remaining option for tribal members who wished to reside on a reduced reservation. Not only did he perceive this solution as economically unfeasible, he also firmly believed that all Indians should be completely free of the BIA. He could not comprehend tribal members choosing to remain affiliated with an organization that had treated them unfairly and unfeelingly.[29]

Only one non-Indian testified at the hearing, John Muench Jr. of the National Forest Products Association. He offered his opinion of the Colville forest resources and recommended against creation of a national forest because it would have a depressive effect on the local economy. Both Ferry and Okanogan counties qualified for aid under the Economic Development Administration, and Muench told the subcommittee that a national forest designation would allow no new opportunities for investment. "It is not consistent with government efforts to encourage regional economic development."[30]

Muench encouraged the subcommittee to allow the tribe to create a development plan that would call for open and competitive bids on the timber, and would allow a multiyear approach. He believed that disposition in a short period of time would hurt the forest products industry and ultimately be a disservice to the Colvilles. The government should educate the Colvilles about the bidding process, Muench suggested, and about methods for choosing the best bid based on several criteria other than strict dollar amount. He considered this instruction the best way to create a stable forest economy for the Colville timber, as well as a sustaining solution to income generation if members chose to remain enrolled in the tribe. Developing the forest resources in this way would also add to the tax base of the counties and soften any burden they encountered as a result of termination.[31]

Mary Lemery, speaking on behalf of the Committee on Indian

Rights, a new group opposed to termination, had the last word at that final hearing on Colville termination. The group had formed since the 1967 hearings, and was largely composed of reservation members. "This group is increasing in number as more tribal members become disenchanted with the movement to liquidate our homeland." From Lemery's perspective, the bill did not provide acceptable financial remuneration for nontangibles such as hunting and fishing rights, subsurface rights, and the potential posed by development of the recreational areas. Her group believed that the forests and lands had been undervalued, and she did not accept the proposition that tribal members should hold a referendum on termination before understanding the financial worth of reservation assets.[32]

Lemery reminded the committee of other nonquantifiable assets. The tribe held paramount usage rights to one quarter of the shoreline along Lake Roosevelt, the reservoir created by Grand Coulee Dam. The tribe had also been promised a share of the revenue generated from the sale of electricity produced by Grand Coulee, and had never received any payment. If they terminated, they would lose the income and the right to go to court in pursuit of a settlement. While the Indian Claims Commission settled disputes of this kind, the Colvilles had never filed a claim for recompense for the power revenue. Attempting to file a claim in the midst of the termination debate would have complicated the matter further and would not have been well received by Congress.[33]

The Committee on Indian Rights wanted federal supervision and the chance to participate in federal programs promoting education, housing improvements, and resource development. They believed that these opportunities provided a better way to improve the individual and tribal economic welfare than termination ever could. Lemery encouraged the committee to act thoughtfully: "We firmly believe that a careful study should be made of the entire subject of termination." She did not want tribal members to suffer as other tribes had suffered because of a few zealous supporters of the legislation.[34]

Fourteen years devoted to careful crafting of termination legislation culminated rather inauspiciously that afternoon in July when Congressman Haley suggested that the committee vote then go to lunch. Congress would continue to consider Colville termination into the 1970s but held no further hearings. It is easy to imagine these tribal members, dressed in their best clothes, tired after a long plane ride, wilting slightly in the humid DC heat. They would have appeared before the subcommittee that day in various states of hope and anxiety, veterans of previous hearings that had led to no decision. After seven years of testimony, they had refined their speeches and arguments, and they endeavored to assert themselves effectively before this group of congressmen assigned to protect their rights.

The hearing record does not report the vote, but history exposed the failure of H.R. 3051 to advance beyond this Subcommittee on Indian Affairs. The Colville Tribes remain on their reservation and in possession of their tribal identity, and the Colville termination battle faded away. It did not end. Neither side emerged victorious because they won the day with skilled arguments and informed conclusions. Instead, momentum took over, and the same body that wanted the end of federal supervision in 1950 had reversed itself by 1970. As the factions of the Colville Reservation gathered their papers, packed away years of work and evidence, and faced each other without this argument to carry forward, they must have wondered what would come next. How strange to be actively engaged with federal policy one day and completely out of step with it the next. Trust the fickle government to change direction again.

The tribal council decision to pursue restoration of the ceded (some tribal members would say stolen) North Half of the Colville Reservation had launched Colville termination. That land, lost through a sale to the federal government that was never honored, represented an important piece of Colville heritage. Three Colville bands historically resided on that land, and before the cession, all tribal members could hunt and fish on that land as part of their "usual and accustomed places." When the tribal council learned that they would recover the North Half if the Colvilles agreed to write a termination plan, it seized the opportunity and, early in the long termination battle, won limited restoration of the North Half. The land was not restored to the reservation base and the tribe was not paid for the original sale, but tribal members could freely access 818,000 acres of the regained North Half, which was a cherished victory.

That victory vindicated the Colvilles' long debate with the government and also prepared them for their future as a leading voice in

Washington State tribal politics. Tribal council members learned how to leverage lawmakers in pursuit of tribal goals, even if community members were not united concerning those goals. Cooperation with politicians and elected officials led to many successful programs on the Colville Reservation, from settlement of the Grand Coulee and Wells dams disputes to increased funding for education, health care, and economic development.

The council leveraged tribal sovereignty to achieve these successes and more. Tribal members who believed that sovereignty could only be achieved by independence from the federal government were unable to imagine how tribal resources would benefit from a government honoring its commitment. When President Richard Nixon repudiated H.C.R. 108 in 1970 and called upon Congress to repeal the policy because it was morally and legally unacceptable, Colville tribal members began to listen.[35] One year later, Ernest Stevens, director of community affairs for the BIA, urged tribal members to fight termination—a reversal of the BIA's previous position. The tribal council held a special meeting in Seattle in April, and Stevens attended to share his perspective on the Colvilles giving up their reservation, "Not another inch, not another drop."[36]

Finally tribal members began to change their minds about Colville termination, and in 1971 they voted an anti-termination majority into the tribal council. Within a year, Lucy Covington would oversee the passage of a council resolution nullifying further consideration of termination. She had fought termination since the beginning, and she remained determined to protect the tribe from any further attempts after she left office.

In the end, the Colville Confederated Tribes had used sovereignty to attain its goals—land restoration and an empowered tribal organization—while still acting as an independent body, not as a puppet of the BIA. The push for termination began in halls and chambers far removed from the Columbia Plateau, but the congressional quest for liquidation resulted in more than just debate for the Colville Tribes. Economics and social politics launched a policy that still affects Indian Country, but the Colvilles focused less on what the policy meant for Indians across the nation and more on how they could use the policy to strengthen the tribal body and to support tribal members.

For tribal members who wanted to keep the reservation, the debate over termination was never about the larger society or the congressional bottom line. It was about working with the federal government to insure tribal advancement and protection, right alongside independence. More than that, though, it was about the land. About restoration. And about home.

CONCLUSION

"We kept getting a little bit smarter."

THE Colville termination battle remained an internal debate, despite outside efforts to influence the outcome. While other tribes, the Bureau of Indian Affairs, national Indian organizations, and members of Congress attempted to move the Colville discussion one way or the other, Colville tribal members controlled the termination conversation. The debates did not occur in a vacuum, however, and many tribal members referenced the Klamath Tribe's and the Menominee Tribe's terminations once those events emerged as illustrative cautionary tales.

The Klamath represented both the nearest and most relevant example, because their forests comprised roughly the same acreage and stumpage as the Colvilles' and because they resided relatively close geographically to the Colville Reservation. The Menominee example became more and more disheartening as that group devolved from being the tribe that owned its power company and some of the best recreational land in the United States to being almost destitute and terribly dependent upon the federal government and the state of Wisconsin.

The Klamath's tribal designation happened in a similar manner as the Colvilles'. The government moved the Klamath, Modoc, and Yahooskin band of Snake Indians onto what became the Klamath Reservation in southwestern Oregon, despite the fact that these groups had not historically been constant friends. By the 1950s, roughly two thousand tribal members identified as Klamaths, and many seemed to fare well in the local economy. According to one source, the county welfare rolls listed only four tribal members in 1957. General assessment of the Klamaths in the early 1950s indicated that about one-third of tribal members lived away from the reservation, and the remainder mixed easily with their non-Indian neighbors.[1] Their perceived economic stability and high degree of acculturation made the Klamaths easy targets for termination. As a result, in 1953 Congress enacted Public Law 587, a bill providing for termination of the Klamath Indians no later than 1962.[2]

Further study of the Klamaths, however, depicted a different reservation than the one described before P.L. 587 became law. The management specialists retained to examine and quantify reservation resources gave Congress the bad news in 1957. They found the general Klamath population less educated than their non-Indian counterparts and less acclimated to the local community than previously asserted. Only 60 percent of the 225 Klamath students in the local schools advanced to the next grade during the school year 1953–54. Only one-third of the adult male population held a steady, full-time job. Ominous foreshadowing lurked in one statement, "Records disclose a number of . . . individuals who have received substantially large sums of cash at various times and have dissipated those sums without apparent increase in their standard of living."[3]

Discussions of dissolving a tribal entity would be troubling in any situation, but in the Klamath case, quickly rising stakes limited the time available for thoughtful consideration. Estimates valued Klamath timber and other resources at an amount that would provide a settlement ranging from $25,000 to $55,000 per person. This would have been a substantial sum in the 1950s—or today—and dreams of money lulled many tribal members into believing that termination would be a good course of action.

Like the Colvilles, the Klamaths did not have one specific heritage or set of traditions. Many arguments that the Colvilles put forth throughout their debate can be found in the Klamath discussions as well. For those who fit well into the dominant community and had, as one Colville tribal member asserted, "left behind the ways of the blanket," choosing to withdraw and liquidate did not pose any cultural quandary. Like urban and off-reservation Colvilles, similar groups of Klamaths felt comfortable enough in non-Indian society to embrace it fully. For others who remained observant of their individual bands' traditions, termination posed more of a problem. The older generation would especially suffer from a rapid termination because most of them faced continual unemployment and lacked the skills necessary to attain steady work. This group naturally depended more heavily on BIA resources than those living away from the reservation, or those living comfortably among their non-Indian neighbors.

Neither the BIA nor the Klamath tribal officials explained the termination process to tribal members, and few tribal members understood what termination would mean for them. A Stanford Research Institute study from 1956 indicated that more than one-third of tribal members felt that they could retain their tribal designation after selling their land. Most did not have any idea why they had been asked to accept termination, and half of the tribal members responding to the question indicated that they did not feel ready for termination as individuals or as a tribe.[4]

Despite widespread misunderstanding of the policy, Klamath termination advanced, and in April of 1958 tribal members voted on whether to withdraw or remain. A total of 1,649 tribal members voted to withdraw, while only 74 elected to remain. Slightly more than four hundred tribal members refused to participate in the vote, and under the rules of P.L. 587, they counted as part of the remaining group. So many more people elected to terminate than anticipated that the BIA had to arrange a larger timber sale in order to accommodate the withdrawing members. This severely reduced the resources of the remaining members and would affect their financial status for years to come.[5] The Klamaths had only one chance to vote on termination, which illustrates how little public education the Klamaths were able to conduct in comparison with the Colvilles.

The Klamaths got a big surprise after they had voted for termination. An appraisal of the tribe's timber assets had been completed prior to the vote, and the appraisers offered a dollar amount of almost $120 million. The Klamaths assumed that they had voted on termination at that price. However, a new bill had been passed in the interim between the original bill and the termination vote that dealt specifically with timber disposition. The new bill called for a complete reevaluation of timber assets after the tribe voted on the original termination bill. The amended timber bill had been designed to protect the purchaser from overpaying in the event of a weakened timber market. The market had fallen significantly since 1953, and by the time the reappraisal had been completed, the value of the Klamath's timber came in at just under ninety-one million dollars.[6]

This discrepancy resulted in a payment of about fifteen thousand dollars less per tribal member than the original amount would have yielded. Not surprisingly, tribal members hotly contested this secret amendment, but to no avail. Congress had enacted it, and the BIA stood by the new requirements. Several Colvilles mentioned this aspect of the Klamath experience during their own hearings in the 1960s, and cautioned others not to trust that the government would honor any dollar amount they provided prior to termination.

Haphazard remains the best way to describe the Klamath termination process. Wade Crawford, a one-time leader of the tribe and ardent advocate of termination, had been pressing for it since the late 1940s. He firmly asserted that all but 2 or 3 percent of the tribe already managed their own affairs and would be unaffected by their change in status. Congress, eager to proceed, listened to Crawford and began to comprehend the full story only after it had approved a termination bill. Klamath tribal members did not get the same opportunity to discuss and understand termination that the Colvilles did, and had only one chance to vote in an election that would be immediately binding.

Additionally, the question of resource valuation never produced the same answer twice, which caused even greater confusion. The legislators, local officials, and heads of the departments of Budget and Agriculture struggled to appraise the value of tribal resources, but they could not. If these men could not produce a definitive solution, imagine how confusing it must have been for the tribal members. Colville tribal members who opposed termination feared a similar lack of preparation and knowledge throughout their debate. Tribal members legitimately questioned how, when the government had been unable to simplify matters for the Klamath, it would be able to do so for the Colvilles. One Klamath tribal member, speaking before the Subcommittee on Indian Affairs at the Klamath termination hearings in 1958, summed up the Klamath situation this way: "The question of timber has been discussed pro and con, but the question of the social implications for the Indian himself has not been dwelled on in these hearings."[7]

The tribal members who desired termination had been wooed by the promise of more money than they had ever seen at once. Local non-Indian communities drummed their fingers excitedly, thinking about the tax revenue the county would enjoy after the land became public land. The timber companies could not wait to acquire the tribal timber at a decent bargain in order to sell it at a large profit later. Many more out-siders expressed a financial interest in the Klamath termination than in the Colville termination, and they certainly influenced the Klamaths in immeasurable ways as a result of their attentions.

In the end, upon their termination in 1961, the Klamaths who termi-nated received a $43,000 payment. Some invested it wisely and enjoyed new homes and educations for their children or themselves, and felt some security about the future. Most, however, spent it fast and on noth-ing of consequence. They returned then, financially and spiritually dis-sipated, only to realize that they no longer had a place to call home. The Klamath Tribe did not exist.

Tribal members and lawyers spent the next twenty-five years fight-ing to regain federal recognition for the Klamath Tribe. In 1986 Con-gress finally passed the Klamath Restoration Act and restored federal services for the Klamaths. The land base remained lost, however, since it had been sold to private parties and was not held by the government. Many tribal members certainly lamented the loss of their home, but they also rejoiced at regaining their name. One terminated Ute tribal member asserted that he never felt divorced from his identity as a Ute after ter-mination. The hard-won Klamath fight to be recognized again remains an indication that they never forfeited their identity either.

Two thousand miles away, in Wisconsin, the Menominee termination process began in 1951, four years after BIA commissioner William Zim-merman had named the group fit to manage their own affairs, but before Congress passed H.C.R. 108, the initial termination bill that started it all. In 1951 the Menominee had been awarded $8.5 million from Congress as a settlement of a Menominee suit for past BIA mismanagement. In response to news of the award, the Menominee Advisory Council began to create an economic development program for the tribe, to augment and improve reservation resources, and they also provided for a $1,000 per capita payment. In 1953 the Menominee General Council, responding to the appeals of tribal members, superceded the advisory council and provided for $1,500 per capita for tribal members. After reviewing their development plan and per capita request, the BIA recommended against passage of both until the Menominee created a comprehensive termina-tion plan, the foundation of which was provided for in H.C.R. 108.[8]

Tribal leaders confronted a difficult choice. On one hand they faced strong pressure from tribal members to win distribution of the per capita payment. On the other, the BIA and Congress had made it plain that there would be no per capita without termination legislation. Generally the Menominee felt prepared to officially take on management responsibility of their reservation businesses. They owned extensive timber resources, a sawmill, utilities, and a small clothing factory. Their income from these industries paid the BIA management costs associated with the Menominee Reservation, and they also had a sizeable cash reserve on deposit with the US Treasury. In 1953 the general council passed a resolution to transfer "supervisory and administrative responsibilities now vested in the federal government" to the Menominee, with the transfer to be completed no later than 1958. However, the council also specifically included a clause indicating that it did not wish to completely end federal supervision over their affairs.[9]

In response to the dual pressures from the BIA and the tribal membership, and because the Menominee wished to have more control of their industries anyway, the tribal leadership reluctantly agreed to draft termination legislation. These leaders did not personally favor termination but felt that they acted in the best interests of tribal members who desired the just distribution of their judgment payment. One leader observed, "The $1,500 share payment was most important to Menominees. [We] figured at the time that we could work on changing things later on."[10]

The Menominees experienced much greater federal pressure to terminate than the Klamaths or the Colvilles did. Senator Arthur Watkins of Utah, who proclaimed to want to "free the Indians" of their federal bondage through terminating their infrastructure and identities, persistently strong-armed the Menominee to terminate. In 1953 Wisconsin congressman Melvin Laird introduced a bill allowing for the $1,500 per capita distribution, and it passed the House of Representatives without objection. A month later, however, Laird and Menominee tribal members had to appear before the Subcommittee on Indian Affairs to make their argument again. They left without a decision. Watkins, chair of the committee at the time, grilled them intently about Menominee preparedness to terminate. In June, Watkins went to the Menominee Reservation and indicated that he would not approve the per capita payment until the Menominee had adopted a program to end federal supervision within three years. One hour later, the general council put a resolution before the membership to end supervision in five years, after the closing of the rolls and appraisal and disposition of assets. The resolution passed 169 to 5, with 28 abstentions.[11]

Rapid passage of such an important resolution indicates how badly the tribal members needed that per capita payment. Tribal lawyers had repeatedly urged the general council to give up on the per capita because the price for obtaining it would be too high. Watkins continued to insist on a three-year termination plan and the Menominee advisory council strongly opposed this amendment to their bill. They asked Laird to reintroduce their five-year plan and to protect them.

The Senate passed the three-year plan, but the House, largely because of Laird's influence, supported the five-year plan. House members felt that they had too little knowledge of the true Menominee position on termination, and they requested hearings to better understand what tribal members wanted. Even after the hearings in March of 1954, the Senate and the House remained stuck to their respective positions. Finally they compromised on a 4.5-year termination plan, and president Dwight D. Eisenhower signed it into law in June of 1954. While the Menominee leadership recognized this as a significant setback, they did not consider it fatal. They had won many battles with the government, and they remained optimistic that they could eventually undo the policy. They also hoped for an administration change in 1956, a swing to a Democratic president, who they believed would have the interests of the Indian in mind.[12]

When faced with the question of termination, the majority of tribal members had no clear understanding of what the policy meant or how it would affect them in the long term. Like many Klamath members, some Menominee thought that they would be able to terminate federal supervision but keep their land and services. Once termination passed, the BIA removed a considerable number of employees from the Menominee agency, which confused tribal members and the general council. The BIA had left the Menominee at the mercy of the subcommittee's goals for implementation of termination, a prospect that it justified by indicating that the Bureau had no further position in the debate once the legislation had passed. When tribal members began to challenge termination and ask for more time to complete the process, the bureau asserted that "the ultimate responsibility for determining when the time has arrived for terminating a federal trust responsibility rests solely with Congress.

The Indians have no vested right to the continuance of the trust relationship." As the planning years went by and tribal members continued to protest against termination, they could eventually point to a promise made by secretary of the Interior Fred Seaton, who in 1958 promised that no termination would proceed without tribal acceptance. In response, the BIA commented that consent only applied to initial termination discussions. Once Congress had passed legislation, the tribe would have no position as to the progress of their termination.[13]

The state of Wisconsin had begun to echo the tribe's concern that the Menominees had not been properly prepared for termination. The state became nervous that it would end up supporting the majority of these tribal members once federal supervision ended. State leaders realized that the tribe's primary source of income, timber, would have to be sold or allocated for sale in order to provide for termination payments. Without that resource for income, the tribe would face severe financial challenges. The state had not actively opposed termination at the crucial moment prior to congressional approval, and that would cost the state government in the long run.[14]

The Menominee Tribe did have a strong financial foundation in the early 1950s. The problem, however, lay in their lack of diversification. They had a number of small industries on their reservation, but they drew their primary financial support from timber and timber-related employment. Mill employees earned roughly $2,300 annually, but non-Indian locals held more than 80 percent of those jobs. Menominee tribal members had a median income of $650 in the period between 1950 and 1954. The Menominee Tribe had 3,059 members, and 80 percent of them lived on tribal land. One-third of Menominees received state assistance, while only one-thirty-sixth of the non-Indian population utilized these benefits. The Menominee tribal members attained roughly the same level of education as the rest of the state but had completed little management training and few job skills workshops. As a result, non-Indians always held the executive positions within the tribal operations. Had the subcommittee truly studied this information, they would never have predicted success for Menominee termination, nor would they have targeted this group in the first place.[15]

In light of all the factors converging to create momentum for Menominee termination—Watkins, pro-termination congressmen, a weak BIA, lack of education about the issue, and state representatives who held no position until too late—the end of federal supervision is not surprising. Menominee termination became complete in 1961.

Termination remains an event of unmatched importance in the Menominee experience, partially because of its reversal relatively soon after Congress had terminated them. A new group emerged after termination, to fight against the tribal leaders who had proposed and overseen termination. A united group of Menominees who wanted termination overturned formed Determination of Rights and Unity for Menominee Shareholders, or DRUMS. Led in large part by Ada Deer,[16] and influenced by the Red Power Movement, DRUMS built their membership base in Milwaukee and Chicago before returning to Menominee County to speak to local tribal members.

After a failed attempt to gain shareholder control of Menominee Enterprises, Incorporated (MEI), in 1971, DRUMS members began running for vacant board positions, and by 1972 held a majority over the former leaders of MEI. As a result, they gained control of the organization using the same approach the Colville Liquidation Promoters utilized when they seized control of the Colville Tribal Council.[17]

With a new group in control of MEI, the Menominee began to strive in earnest to restore recognition to the tribe. They did not want to be ruled by the same paternalistic bureau that had sacrificed them to Congress, but instead wanted a more equitable relationship that allowed the Menominee greater control. DRUMS sought repeal of the Menominee Termination Act and inauguration of self-determination for the tribe. When Congress passed the Menominee Restoration Act in 1973, it met most of DRUMS' requirements. Menominee restoration proved an enormously important turning point for Congress. Only four members of the House of Representatives voted against restoration, which indicates how far lawmakers had retreated from termination in twenty years.[18]

DRUMS' importance is not limited to the Menominee. Seen in the context of the Red Power Movement, both as a product of it and as a force within it, DRUMS brought pride and newfound identity back to Indians across the United States. The success of DRUMS and the Menominee Restoration Act laid the foundation for Klamath restoration thirteen years later. DRUMS provided an example for a better way, a more sophisticated way, to deal with the BIA.

Three other termination experiences offer additional context for the termination era as well as for the Colville process. The Confederated Salish and Kootenai Tribes of Montana avoided termination because their state politicians actively opposed it; the mixed-blood Utes of Utah fell to termination at the hands of their fellow tribal members; and the Coos, Lower Umpqua, and Siuslaw Indians of Oregon won hard-fought recognition of a land claim just as the termination era began, and then were terminated along with fifty-eight other tribal groups in Western Oregon.

The Confederated Salish and Kootenai Tribes defeated termination primarily because of support from their congressional and local representatives. While a few elected officials in Montana initially thought termination a good theory, they rejected it after they became more educated about the Salish and Kootenai situation. State officials especially expressed concern that the state would bear the brunt of increased administration and welfare costs if the Salish and Kootenai lost federal supervision. While termination would put more land into the tax base, state officials did not believe that the increased revenue would balance the new expenses of supporting Salish and Kootenai tribal members.

County officials, on the other hand, advocated termination for the Salish and Kootenai early in their termination discussions. At the local level, many Montana residents perceived Salish and Kootenai tribal members to be highly acculturated and felt that they would have no trouble adapting to life without federal supervision. Of course, many ranchers and farmers wanted to see the end of the "special rights" the Salish and Kootenai ranchers enjoyed. These locals believed that the removal of federal supervision would create a more equitable playing field for everyone and would ultimately help the Salish and Kootenai value their land and vocations.

Unlike their Montana peers, elected officials in the state of Washington did not oppose termination. Instead, state and national congressmen lent their support to Colville termination, many of them introducing termination bills at the behest of the Colvilles. Local officials from Ferry and Okanogan counties, the two counties within reservation boundaries, also favored termination and did not believe that they would suffer any unmanageable expenses when federal supervision of the Colvilles ended. The counties happily anticipated an increased tax base, and many county officials believed that the majority of Colvilles would scatter permanently once they received a liquidation payment. County administrators concluded that the tax revenue would more than compensate for any expense incurred as a result of tribal members needing welfare assistance and other county services.[19]

The Salish and Kootenai also credited their legal counsel with defeating termination. Salish and Kootenai attorneys devoted years to reviewing treaties and working with both the tribe and the BIA to prevent Salish and Kootenai termination. Their persistence, and the strong opposition of local tribal members to termination, protected the Flathead Reservation and the Salish and Kootenai. Because of the input from counsel, elected officials' resistance to termination, and the united opposition to termination presented by the six other Indian tribes in Montana, the Subcommittee on Indian Affairs defeated the Flathead (Salish and Kootenai) termination bill at its 1954 hearing. Senator Watkins tried to reintroduce it during the second session that year, but Senator James Murray of Montana blocked it, and the bill died, never to reappear.[20]

This example provides another direct contrast to the Colville experience. The Colville attorney, Joseph Wicks, who first offered commentary on Colville termination in 1965, did not believe Colville tribal members when they asserted their desire to remain Indian. His conclusion stemmed from their use of trucks instead of horses and the prevalence of televisions across the reservation. He told the Subcommittee on Indian Affairs, as well as anyone else who would listen, that the Colvilles could survive termination and that it should happen as quickly as possible.[21] Wicks had been retained during the pro-termination majority on the tribal council, so he listened to them when they told him that the Colvilles desired termination. However, it would have been obvious to even the most casual observer that Wicks did not try to balance the needs of both sides of this debate.

More interesting in the context of the Colville termination debates is the fact that the Flathead bill had only one hearing. While the majority of the Salish and Kootenai did not favor termination, a large group of off-reservation residents wanted it and fought for it. The Salish amd Kootenai experience, then, shared a similar on-reservation/off-reservation divide, but off-reservation Colvilles were much more organized in their pursuit of termination and had a strong chance of winning the battle. The Colville Indian Association, largely an off-reservation group, organized first in pursuit of termination, followed closely by the Colville Liquidation Promoters on the reservation. Once the CLP gained control of the tribal council, its goal aligned with the CIA's position, and the two groups each continued to introduce bills to the Subcommittee on Indian Affairs. The Salish and Kootenai had to defeat only one bill to escape termination. Colville tribal members' resistance led to defeat of nearly a dozen in two houses.

The mixed-blood Uintah Utes of Utah may have suffered most cruelly from the termination experience because, although the government had originally marked their whole tribal group for termination, only the mixed-bloods completed the process. Their full-blood cohorts sacrificed them in order to preserve the tribe and the Ute land base. Senator Arthur Watkins targeted the Uncompahgre, Whiteriver, and Uintah Utes for termination in 1950, and charged them with creating a long-range termination plan. As with Menomiee termination, this demand closely followed a large settlement that the Utes had received from the government. Watkins and the BIA viewed the settlement as reason enough for the tribes to become self-sufficient, and Watkins especially wanted Indians from his home state to serve as examples for the benefits of termination. Watkins told the community that unless they complied with drafting a withdrawal plan, he would withhold part of the settlement until they did. The tribes did not like the inequity of this proposition, but agreed to it in order to gain the judgment money rightly belonging to them.

Like the Colvilles and the Klamaths, these three Ute bands had not always been one tribe, and consequently did not always enjoy the same vision for tribal living or governance. The government relocated the Uintah Utes onto the land base of the other two bands. In their new home, the Uintahs continued their past habits of adopting Indians of other tribes into their tribe. They also adopted whites they considered in possession of Indian values. The Uncompahgre and Whiteriver bands frowned upon this practice but did not attempt to influence the Uintahs in any significant way. The three tribes generally enjoyed good relationships and cohabitated well together. While the Uintahs continued to welcome others into their tribe and onto their land, the Uncompahgre and the Whiteriver maintained more insular ties and married mostly within their respective tribes. The BIA treated them as one tribal group and this posed no problem until the twin events of the eighteen-million-dollar judgment award and the press for termination occurred.

The BIA allocated funds equally among the three tribes, or as one tribal group. The tribes faced a decision about the management of the funds. Some wanted a simple per capita disbursement, but the bureau indicated that it would not support an unrestricted payout of that kind. Instead, it encouraged the tribes to create a three-year improvement and rehabilitation program, which would be partially funded by the judgment. The BIA also indicated that the tribe should begin long-range planning to end federal supervision.[22] The tribes had no choice but to accept what the BIA would give them—permission for a per capita payout if they created a termination plan. This moment represents the beginning of the end of tribal unity.

Over the next three years, tribal planning committee officials and tribal members observed the results of the three-year improvement plan and wondered about the simple per capita payment. They did not act on Watkins's long-range plan for withdrawal until Robert Bennett, an Oneida Indian and BIA programming officer, visited the reservation. At this point, Bennett essentially acted as messenger for Watkins; he reminded the planning committee that Watkins meant to enforce their earlier agreement regarding payment of the judgment. Watkins needed an example for his vision of termination, and he intended for the Utes to provide it. Furthermore, although Bennett belonged to an Indian community, he believed that Indians would fare better without the interference of the BIA. Consequently he supported termination.

The planning committee began to host open meetings on the results of the three-year program and the possibility of the withdrawal of federal supervision. In 1952 tribal members complained that each person did not receive an equal benefit from the three-year program. Many asserted that the mixed-blood Uintahs benefited more than others in the tribe. The mixed-bloods already enjoyed a high degree of acculturation and familiarity with economic development and business ideas promoted in the three-year program due to a long tradition of intermarriage and intermixing with the dominant society. Members of the Uncompahgre and Whiteriver bands did not think it fair that the Uintahs used the majority of the three-year program benefits and would still get an equal share in the per capita payment promised in return for termination legislation.

Just after New Year's Day in 1954, leaders of the Uncompahgre band approached Francis McKinley, a leader of the tribal planning board, and proposed a program of division that would separate their assets from the other two bands. McKinley appreciated their perspective, but he could not alienate other members of the board. Shortly afterward, McKinley attended the NCAI conference and ran into Bennett. He told Bennett of the Uncompahgre proposal, and Bennett seized on it as a possible solution. Bennett joined McKinley and Rex Curry, another planning board leader, on the reservation to propose a division of the three bands, but the other two bands objected. The three officials then concluded that perhaps instead of separating the bands from each other, Curry and McKinley could propose to delineate between full-bloods and mixed-bloods.[23]

All three men perceived this to be the solution to the looming threat of termination. The full-bloods and the integrity of the tribe would be protected, while the mixed-bloods would be terminated to satisfy Watkins demands. The planning committee held a general tribal meeting on March 31, 1954, to vote on their new blood quantum parameter—anyone with less than 50 percent Indian blood would be terminated. Only four hundred tribal members attended the meeting that day (23 percent of the tribe), few of them mixed-bloods. The debate proved confusing, and many did not fully understand the premise of the vote or that their vote would be binding. Most believed that they were simply indicating how they would vote when the vote arrived, and that day the overwhelming majority agreed with the idea of dividing membership between full-blood and mixed-blood tribal members. Bennett took the vote results back to Watkins and then they drafted legislation reflecting the so-called Ute partition. Congress passed it in April without objection and forced the mixed-bloods toward termination. The BIA published the final mixed-blood rolls in April of 1956, and from that point on, 490 Utes had to begin to plan for termination within five years.[24] When they did terminate in 1961, each member received $4,500 in compensation—a paltry sum for giving up their heritage.[25]

The mixed-bloods represented roughly 27 percent of the total tribal population. Their departure from the rolls and resource base meant expanded services and per capita payments for the remaining members. Watkins still demanded a termination plan from the full-blood members, but by the time they had created one, the federal drive for termination had peaked. The full-bloods thus escaped termination altogether. Unlike the Klamath and the Menominee, the mixed-blood Utes have not been able to regain tribal recognition, but Warren Metcalf indicated that that did not prevent them from identifying themselves as Indian. One terminated mixed-blood characterized it this way, "To me, termination was a government idea. It was an Anglo idea. . . . I never felt myself cut off from being a Ute Indian. I may have been cut off from federal services, but I was never cut off from being an Indian, more particularly a Ute Indian."[26]

Of all the termination experiences, that of the Coos, Lower Umpqua, and Siuslaw Indians of Oregon remains the most complex. Throughout the early twentieth century, the Coos, Lower Umpqua, and Siuslaw group engaged Congress and the BIA in pursuit of official recognition. They had been party to the 1855 Empire Treaty, which was signed, then lost and unratified, then rediscovered among federal documents in Washington, D.C, during a tribal member's visit in 1916. Even though oral tradition recounted the treaty signing and treaty rights, the federal government did not recognize the Coos, Lower Umpqua, and Siuslaw Indians as a formal Indian tribe or group, nor had the government paid the Indians for 1.8 million acres lost as a result of the treaty. In 1918 the Coos, Lower Umpqua, and Siuslaw filed a request to bring suit against the government in the US Court of Claims, to compel recognition. Congress waited eleven years to approve the suit, which forced a loss of momentum supporting the Coos, Lower Umpqua, and Siuslaw effort. Nearly a decade of testimony from the Indians and their non-Indian neighbors illuminated the length of Coos, Lower Umpqua, and Siuslaw occupancy and use of the land. The compilation of reports on how the Government Accountability Office and other offices engaged with the Indians separately from other tribal groups in the area proved the group's assertion that they were not part of the Grand Ronde or Siletz reservations. During this time, the Coos, Lower Umpqua, and Siuslaw also debated whether to organize their tribal government under the Wheeler-Howard Act (IRA). While they ultimately did not accept the Indian Reorganization Act, the discussion represents a certain indicator that they acted as an autonomous tribal group with a government-to-government relationship.

However, in 1938, twenty years after the suit was filed, the court ruled that the evidence presented, including the unratified treaty, was not enough to prove that the Coos, Lower Umpqua, and Siuslaw Indians had governmental recognition of title to lands described in the treaty, and also found that oral tradition was not enough to prove that the group had occupied the land from "time immemorial."[27] In 1951 and 1952 the Coos, Lower Umpqua, and Siuslaw Indians tried to renew their suit before the Indian Claims Commission but were rejected both times, because the ICC believed that the court of claims had given the matter adequate consideration, and that the commission could do no more.[28]

Even as the government continued to deny official recognition of the Coos, Lower Umpqua, and Siuslaw Indians, the tribe still ended up caught in the crossfire of termination. Locked out of proceedings and informational sessions by neighbors such as the Siletz Tribe and Grand Ronde Tribe, who favored termination, but lumped in with these groups by the BIA, the Coos, Lower Umpqua, and Siuslaw did not have a voice in termination proceedings or processes. They opposed termination but were not heard on the subject, and their names were included in the 1954 termination bill removing federal responsibility over sixty-one tribal groups along the Oregon coast, which went into final effect in 1966.[29]

The Coos, Lower Umpqua, and Siuslaw Indians remained committed, despite consistent rejection of their requests and claims, to regaining recognition and reversing their termination. The tribe leveraged local resources, getting letters of support for restoration from non-Indian neighbors throughout the region. They held local meetings about the issue, and raised money through rummage sales and fry bread stands. They worked closely with attorneys and gathered funds to buy a photocopier to produce even more letters and paperwork for a federal government that seemed to thrive on a paper trail. One tribal member said of this acquisition and its attendant practices, "We kept getting a little bit smarter."[30]

Finally, in 1984, Congress passed the Coos, Lower Umpqua, and Siuslaw Restoration Act. One tribal member expressed his joy this way: "We were orphans; now this puts us back in the family of nations."[31] The Coos, Lower Umpqua, and Siuslaw Indians were driven to gain the recognition denied them because of poorly managed administrative details at the federal level. Fighting for decades to remain visible, members of the tribe simply added restoration to their list of goals alongside recognition and fair treatment. The tenacity of tribal members in the mid- to late twentieth century led to both the recognition and the restoration of the Coos, Lower Umpqua, and Siuslaw tribes, and they remain one of the nine federally recognized tribes in Oregon.

Each of these stories illustrates the complexities of a poorly designed and arbitrarily enforced federal policy. Termination represented the final forced federal attempt at assimilating Native Americans into the broader culture. The political push by Congress for termination resonates with previous social justifications of "helping the Indian live in the twentieth century" and "getting the Indian out of the reservation and into society." Termination was also about money. Congressional supporters of the movement were weary of supporting a population of nations within the

United States. They wanted to end federal support not just to free Indians but also to liberate the congressional budget. This maneuvering is evident in the early selection of perceived "wealthy" tribes, such as the Menominee and the Klamath, for termination. Ultimately, the termination processes proved expensive, and tribes needed congressional support during the years leading to termination and in the years following it, so Congress spent more money on Indians than if it had not initiated the process.

Like previous federal policies, termination was designed without input from the tribes. Most tribes targeted for termination vocally opposed it, which is what makes the Colville pursuit of termination so interesting. Despite being clearly out of step with the national Indian scene, Colville elected officials and tribal members on and off the reservation pursued termination for nearly twenty years. The pursuit began with a desire to reclaim the lost North Half of the reservation. That goal was reached almost immediately, however, so what drove the years of struggle, dissension, and frustration?

This question seems simple, but is in fact quite complex. Which tribal member would you ask this of, from what band, in what year? Where does this tribal member live—on the reservation or off, on an allotment or on reservation land or fee land? The complexities of this question manifested in even more complicated answers, and the answers led to formations of alliances that developed, dissolved, and re-formed throughout the Colville termination era.

The end of the Colville termination debates did not come about through one action or event. Instead, years' worth of factors and experience combined to thwart pro-terminationists: the Menominee and the Klamath termination experiences were widely acknowledged to be disastrous; the Klamath did not receive the payments that had been promised; the BIA refused to pass legislation not approved by a majority of members eligible to vote on the issue; and the national mood changed.

When the anti-terminationists won control of the Colville Business Council and passed the resolution prohibiting future termination bills to be submitted by the council, something interesting happened—almost nothing. When witnessing a spectacle, we are caught up in the movement of it, the theater, and when it is over, nothing is left but to walk away. After nearly two decades of fighting, tribal members walked away from the fight and moved on.

They engaged with many programs coming out of the self-determination era and elevated the tribe's potential. The 1971 and 1972 tribal councils made great strides toward self-determination for the Colvilles. Those councils inaugurated the entity that would become the Colville Tribal Enterprises Corporation, the corporation that still manages tribal businesses today. More than nine thousand people are enrolled in the Colville Tribes, almost one hundred percent more than during the 1960s, although the distribution of off-reservation versus reservation membership remains at roughly the same percentage. Tribal members have gone to college and business school and graduate school, and many have returned to the reservation to work for the tribe. These advances reflect well on the entire tribe, and the tribal membership stands to benefit from future results of these enhancements.

The sophistication developed by the tribal members during the termination era would ultimately serve the tribe well. The *Tribal Tribune* continues to be the paper of record for the Colvilles. The political jockeying in the 1960s trained a generation of Colvilles to manage relationships with elected officials, at both the state and national levels. The tribe also quickly renewed relationships with regional and national Indian organizations in the 1970s, and remains a relevant participant in these organizations.

It should be no surprise that a group arbitrarily thrown together by a government seeking convenient solutions did not wish to remain intact. It would be nice to conclude that the termination era brought the bands and tribal members together in support of one cause and one another, but that was not the case. The bands within the Colville Confederated Tribes do not always get along with one another or with their tribal counterparts across the country, but that does not make their opinions any less valid, any less meaningful, or any less important. After all, many Colvilles fought for twenty years for the right to continue to disagree.

APPENDIX

Appendix. Major Legislation Affecting the Colville Confederated Tribes

Legislation	Year	Created by	Central points
Public Law 772	1956	Colville Business Council	Restoration of 818,000 acres of the North Half of the Colville Indian Reservation. Passage of restoration will be followed by creation of a plan to terminate the Colville Confederated Tribes within five years of enactment.
House Resolution 8469	1961*	Colville Business Council	Two-step termination process, closure of tribal rolls upon passage of law by Congress, valuation of tribal and reservation resources, and removal of federal supervision in a time frame to be agreed upon by tribe and BIA.
House Resolution 6801	1962	Colville Indian Assoc.	Complete liquidation of timber assets in preparation for termination, one-step termination of Colville Confederated Tribes, but with an option for tribal members to remain on tribal land if desired.
Senate Bill 1442	1963	Colville Business Council	Initially the same as H.R. 8469, it featured a two-step termination process, closure of tribal rolls upon passage of the law by Congress, valuation of tribal and reservation resources, and removal of federal supervision in a time frame to be agreed upon by tribe and BIA. By the end of the 1963 Subcommittee on Indian Affairs hearings, it would be revised to feature a one-step termination process.

House Resolution 4918	1963	Colville Indian Assoc.	Complete liquidation of timber assets in preparation for termination, one-step termination of Colville Confederated Tribes, no provision for post-termination hunting and fishing rights, termination could be passed by majority of tribal members voting in termination referendum.
House Resolution 5925 / Senate 1413	1965	Colville Business Council	One-step termination process, closure of tribal rolls upon passage of law by Congress, valuation of tribal and reservation resources, and removal of federal supervision in a time frame to be agreed upon by tribe and BIA, but also including an option to remain as a tribal corporation for tribal members who did not wish to accept a cash payout. Termination could be approved by majority of tribal members voting in termination referendum.
House Resolution 6631	1965	Colville Indian Assoc.	Complete liquidation of timber assets in preparation for termination, one-step termination of Colville Confederated Tribes, no provision for post-termination hunting and fishing rights, termination could be passed by majority of tribal members voting in termination referendum.
Senate Bill 282	1967	Colville Business Council	One-step termination process, closure of tribal rolls upon passage of law by Congress, valuation of tribal and reservation resources, and seven-year time frame for removal of federal supervision for those tribal members who did not wish to accept an immediate cash payout. Termination could be passed by majority of tribal members voting in termination referendum.
Senate Bill 282 / HR 3051	1968	Colville Business Council	One-step termination process, closure of tribal rolls upon passage of law by Congress, valuation of tribal and reservation resources, and seven-year time frame for removal of federal supervision for those tribal members who did not wish to accept an immediate cash payout. Termination could be passed by majority of tribal members voting in termination referendum.

*Tabled by Subcommittee on Interior and Insular Affairs until 1962, and again until 1963.

NOTES

Book epigraph: The sentiments of members of the San Poil band of Colville Indians as conveyed to their Indian agent, John McAdams Webster, in 1906. While the comments reference the recent sale of the North Half of the Colville Indian Reservation, they also perfectly represent issues of contention that would pervade the Colville termination debates half a century later: land, money, tribal membership, and rejection of federal government oversight. "Letter from John McAdams Webster, Indian Agent, Captain, U.S. Army, to George M. Anderson, Special Attorney, Department of Justice," November 5, 1906. John McAdams Webster Papers (cage 145, container 2, folder 5), Manuscripts, Archives, and Special Collections (MASC), Holland and Terrell Libraries, Washington State University, Pullman, WA.

PREFACE

1 House Concurrent Resolution 108 was introduced by Senator Henry M. Jackson and passed during the 83rd Congress, August 1, 1953 (H. Con. Res. 108), 67 Stat. B122.

2 Donald L. Fixico, *Termination and Relocation: Federal Indian Policy, 1945–1960* (Albuquerque: University of New Mexico Press, 1986); Kenneth R. Philp, *Termination Revisited: American Indians on the Trail to Self-Determination, 1933–1953* (Lincoln: University of Nebraska Press, 1999).

3 Jaakko Puisto. "'This Is My Reservation, I Belong Here': The Salish Kootenai Struggle Against Termination" (PhD diss., Arizona State University, 2000); R. Warren Metcalf, *Termination's Legacy: The Discarded Indians of Utah* (Lincoln: University of Nebraska Press, 2002); David R. M. Beck, *Seeking Recognition: The Termination and Restoration of the Coos, Lower Umpqua, and Siuslaw Indians, 1855–1984* (Lincoln: University of Nebraska Press, 2009); Nicholas C. Peroff, *Menominee DRUMS: Tribal Termination and Restoration, 1954–1974* (Norman: University of Oklahoma Press, 1982).

4 Members of the Colville Confederated Tribes often refer to "the Tribe" and "the Tribes" interchangeably, and also often use "Colvilles" to describe themselves and other tribal members. I use these terms interchangeably throughout the text as well, and this varied usage is consistent with standard practices among tribal members. The same is true for references to band names, such as "Nespelems," "Okanogans," and so on.

5 See http://www.colvilletribes.com. To date, no scholarly history of the Colville

Confederated Tribes has been published. Some self-published works include aspects of Colville history, and many other works reference events such as the McLaughlin Agreement and Chief Joseph joining the Colville tribes, but I privilege the Colville tribes' account over other accounts, and consider the history recounted on this website as correct.

1. "WE WANT TO BE INDIANS FOREVER."

1 Territorial governor Isaac Stevens had negotiated treaties in the 1850s, the most famous regionally being the Yakama Treaty in 1855, but had never made his way as far as the northern Columbia Plateau. The bands on the plateau escaped a treaty in return for the promise not to participate in wars against the United States. While Stevens planned to return to the plateau, the Civil War shunted aside US concerns about diplomacy with Indians. Many small bands of Indians throughout Washington State escaped treaty negotiations altogether. The government viewed these smaller bands, who numbered only a few hundred members, as nonthreatening both because of their size and because they did not tend to unite as one large group. Due to their size, Stevens's schedule, and the fact that after the Civil War the government decided not to treat with Indians any longer, the Colville Indians were among tribes bound by executive order reservations.

2 English names for the bands within the Colville Tribes will be used throughout this study. The Colville Confederated Tribes business council and business operations, as well as most tribal members, consistently use the English band names instead of the Salish or Sahaptian band names.

3 Hudson's Bay Company built a trading post at Kettle Falls, a major trading center, in 1820, although the men employed by HBC had already been trading with indigenous groups before construction of the post.

4 The first Catholic mission in the area, St. Paul's Mission, was established in the 1830s, and was built to serve the HBC population as well as to convert Colville Indians to Catholicism.

5 The Okanogan band on the Colville Reservation is sometimes called Southern Okanogan, because there is also a band of Okanogan Indians in British Columbia, Canada, just across the border from the original Colville Reservation.

6 Chief Moses lived on his own reservation, adjacent to the Colville Reservation, land set aside for him after successful negotiations with the US government. As he began to spend more time on the Colville Reservation and to reside less frequently on his own, he requested that the government allow him to move onto the Colville Reservation and he ceded his own land back to the United States. In exchange, the government relocated him to the area near present-day Nespelem (at the government's expense), paid Moses for his land, and also reportedly gave him an annual stipend. It is easy to understand the Colvilles' frustration at this turn of events, since they had no negotiating power of their own, and certainly received no compensation from the government for the addition of the Moses-Columbia band to the reservation.

7   In John Alan Ross, "Factionalism on the Colville Reservation" (PhD diss., Washington State University, 1967), 67.

8   The Wenatchi and the Palus had ties to the Chelan, Methow and Entiat bands.

9   This kind of intervention was not unique to the Colvilles. The agency ledgers listing farm implements given to individuals and describing the agent's frustration when the Indians lost or traded those implements make for interesting and amusing reading. The National Archives and Records Administration (Pacific Coast Branch, Record Group 75) has several excellent examples of ledger accounts from the Colville Reservation.

10 "Tribe Debates Termination," *Spokesman-Review* (Spokane, WA), March 4, 1964.

11 John McAdams Webster Papers, cage 145, container 2, folder 5, Washington State University, Holland and Terrell Libraries, Manuscripts, Archives, and Special Collections (MASC), Pullman, WA, "Interrogation of Chief Barnaby of the Colville Reservation by John M. Johnson, Clerk and Acting Agent of the Colville Agency," October 16, 1906; "Letter from John McAdams Webster to the Commissioner of Indian Affairs," July 8, 1907.

12 John McAdams Webster Papers, cage 145, container 2, folder 5, WSU HTSC "Letter from John McAdams Webster, Indian Agent, Captain, U.S. Army, to George M. Anderson, Special Attorney, Department of Justice," November 5, 1906.

13 Frederick Hoxie, *A Final Promise: The Campaign to Assimilate the Indians, 1880–1920* (Lincoln: Bison Books for University of Nebraska Press, 2001), 47, 51. The 1891 North Half negotiation was based on the principles of allotment. Throughout the contact period, and especially after the establishment of the federal government, non-Indian pursuit of Indian lands was a high priority. As the US government sought to find both more land for newly arriving settlers and to manage indigenous populations, it vacillated between isolating indigenous peoples from settler communities and forcing indigenous peoples to live among settlers. Henry L. Dawes, US senator, through creation and sponsorship of the General Allotment Act of 1887 (also called the Dawes Act), sought to assimilate Indians rather than isolate them, as the reservation system had done. He determined that reservation lands should be carved into parcels—160 acres or 80 acres—and first be allotted to the Indians on the designated reservations, with the balance of the parcels sold to any qualified buyer. Dawes concluded that once Indians observed the superior habits and practices of non-Indians, the Indians would certainly fall in line with the dominant cultural practices. For more on the Dawes Commission, see also Kent Carter, *The Dawes Commission and the Allotment of the Five Civilized Tribes, 1893–1914* (Orem: UT, Ancestry Publishing, 1999), and Brian W. Dippie, *The Vanishing American: White Attitudes and U.S. Indian Policy* (Lawrence: University Press of Kansas, 1991), 161–76.

14 McLaughlin would have arrived at the meeting armed with the 1903 Lone Wolf v. Hitchcock Supreme Court decision. Many Colvilles remained angry about the government's tactics in obtaining permission to cede the North Half, but Lone Wolf reinforced the legal foundation of the cession. Lone Wolf, a Kiowa named in the suit on behalf of the Kiowas and the Comanches, brought suit asserting that land cessions would be legal and enforceable only if three-fourths of the adult male

population of a tribe had approved the cession. The suit claimed the cession invalid because the three-fourths requirement had not been met. The court ruled that Congress retained plenary power to abrogate sections of treaties, in this case Article 12 of the Treaty of Medicine Creek Lodge of 1867, and that congressional authority remained a political power, not a judicial one (Francis Paul Prucha, *The Great Father: The United States Government and the American Indians* [Lincoln: University of Nebraska Press, 1995], 775–76). For more on Lone Wolf v. Hitchcock and federal Indian policy, see Frank Pommersheim, *Broken Landscapes: Indians, Indian Tribes, and the Constitution* (New York: Oxford University Press, 2009), and Blue Clark, *Indian Tribes of Oklahoma: A Guide*, Civilization of the American Indian series (Norman: University of Oklahoma Press, 2009).

15 The Indian Reorganization Act, also called the Wheeler–Howard Act for its two initial sponsors, Senator Burton K. Wheeler of Montana and Congressman Edgar Howard of Nebraska, was created under the jurisdiction of John Collier, commissioner of Indian Affairs when the IRA was conceived. Some critics say he was too ambitious in his pursuit of Indian input and cultural adherence; others say he did not go far enough to observe tribal values. See Prucha, *Great Father*, 957–63; Peter Iverson, *"We Are Still Here": American Indians in the Twentieth Century* (Wheeling, IL: Harlan Davidson, 1998), 89–98; William E. Leuchtenburg, *Franklin D. Roosevelt and The New Deal* (New York: Harper Perennial, 1963), 86, 326.

16 Inspired by the CIA's enthusiasm, superintendent of Indian Affairs Dillon S. Myer and Commissioner Collier would not give up on the Indians who favored a constitutional government, and both provided assistance in creating a Colville constitution. Collier assured tribal members that a good tribal government would represent "every interest within the tribe … the old people as well as the young, the fullbloods as well as the mixed-bloods," and he promised that no one person within the tribal government would have too much say. Still, few outside the CIA supported the idea of one government, although many requested to be allowed to form individual governments along band lines. Collier would not allow such a fragmented approach, and he insisted that the groups work together to author one constitution representative of all tribal members. During the constitutional debates, splits emerged along band lines, blood quantum, and the eternal designation of the Moses-Columbia band and the Nez Perce band as different from the rest of the kinship bands. These same issues would echo throughout the termination debate.

17 The CIA incorporated under Washington State law in 1956.

18 Quoted in "A History of the Colville Indian Reservation and Its Indian Peoples," Alexandra Harmon, manuscript commissioned by the Colville Confederated Tribes Business Council (n.p., n.d.).

19 Omak, Nespelem, and Inchelium each elect four council members, and Keller elects two, for a total of fourteen council members. Members serve two-year terms, but elections are held annually because each district has only half of its seats open at a time. The council members elect one of the fourteen to serve as chairman of the council. Tribal members are not involved in the selection of the chair.

20 Council member Darlena "Doll" Watt, speech by author commemorating the 125th

anniversary of the Colville Tribes at Nespelem, July 11, 1997, author's collection.

21 The Indian Claims Commission grew out of the old Court of Claims, created in 1855. Members of Congress and officials in the know about Indian affairs realized early in the twentieth century that the Court of Claims could not hear all of the claims Indian groups began to file. In 1929, alongside consideration of greater issues in Indian Country, Commissioner of Indian Affairs Charles J. Rhoads recommended the creation of a special commission to hear land claims and treaty violation claims. Conceived as a US Court of Indian Claims under Rhoads, the idea gained little traction. Once John Collier became commissioner of Indian Affairs, he worked with secretary of the Interior Harold Ickes to create a commission to hear Indian claims, rather than a court. Still, it took seventeen years for Rhoads's idea to become a reality. When President Truman signed it into law in August 1946, he asserted his hope that "with the final settlement of all outstanding claims which this measure insures, Indians can take their place without special handicaps or special advantages in the economic life of our nation and share fully in its progress." Prucha, *Great Father*, 926, 1017–23. For more on the Indian Claims Commission, see Harvey D. Rosenthal, *Their Day in Court: A History of the Indian Claims Commission* (New York: Garland Publishing, 1990); Imre Sutton, ed., *Irredeemable America: The Indians' Estate and Land Claims* (Albuquerque: University of New Mexico Press, 1985).

22 National Archives and Records Administration, Washington, DC, branch (hereafter NARA DC), Record Group 75, Colville 054, Central Classified File 2 (hereafter RG 75, Colville, CCF 2), box 21, folder 00-1953-054, part 1, Colville, "Colville Agenda Colville Business Council with Commission Glenn L. Emmons Yakima, Washington," p. 2.

23 The business council began pursuit of restoration by the late 1940s, but the process really became formalized in the early 1950s.

24 Documents collected at NARA DC, RG 75, Colville, CCF 2, boxes 20–22, bear out this assertion. Specific documents will be cited throughout this work, as appropriate.

25 NARA DC, RG 75, Colville 054, CCF 2, box 21, folder 00-1953-054, part 1, "Colville Agenda Colville Business Council with Commission Glenn L. Emmons Yakima, Washington," p. 1.

26 House Concurrent Resolution 108, introduced by Senator Henry M. Jackson and passed during the 83rd Congress, August 1, 1953 (H. Con. Res. 108), 67 Stat. B122.

27 NARA DC, RG 75, Colville 054, CCF 2, box 21, folder 00-1953-054, part 1, "Colville Agenda Colville Business Council with Commission Glenn L. Emmons Yakima, Washington," p. 5.

28 H.C.R. 108 as introduced to Congress on June 9, 1953, listed the Indian tribes within the states of California, Florida, Iowa, New York, and Texas, and named the following tribes in other states as additional groups to be withdrawn from federal supervision: the Flathead Tribe of Montana, the Klamath Tribe of Oregon, the Menominee Tribe of Wisconsin, the Osage Tribe of Oklahoma, the Potowatami Tribe of Kansas and Nebraska, the Colville Tribe of Washington, and members of the Chippewa Tribe residing on the Turtle Mountain Reservation in North Dakota. The bill was later amended to remove the Colville Tribe and the Osage Tribe from the list of targets, and that bill passed as amended on August 1, 1953.

29 David R. M. Beck, *Seeking Recognition: Termination and Restoration of the Coos, Lower Umpqua, and Siuslaw Indians, 1855–1984* (Lincoln: University of Nebraska Press, 2009), 137–81. The Siletz were restored in 1977.

30 In tribal politics, this is a relatively small number. In *Menominee DRUMS*, Nicholas Peroff outlines the eight factions operating within the Menominee community in their lead up to termination. The Menominee divided along blood, religious, geographic, marriage, and political lines, and several of these divisions had subdivisions. Nicholas C. Peroff. *Menominee DRUMS: Tribal Termination and Restoration, 1954–1974* (Norman: University of Oklahoma Press, 1982), 97–101. Angela Morrill, in her masters thesis, "Decolonizing Klamath Termination: Factionalism in Klamath Termination Discourse," identifies factionalism as a colonial construct that non-Indians in power used against the Klamath Tribe. In her analysis, factionalism became a tool for the dominant culture to depict Indians as savage and unsophisticated, unable to comprehend termination or to get along well enough to fight it. This assessment offers an interesting recasting of the Klamath termination experience but does not apply in the Colville case.

31 See R. Warren Metcalf, *Termination's Legacy: The Discarded Indians of Utah* (Lincoln: University of Nebraska Press, 2002); Susan Hood, "Termination of the Klamath Tribe in Oregon," *Ethnohistory* 19 (Fall 1972): 379–92.

32 NARA DC, RG 75, Colville 054, CCF 2, Box 21, folder 00-1953-054, part 1, "Colville Minutes Special Session of the Colville Business Council, May 27 & 28, 1954, Colville Indian Agency." Also, "Colville Commercial Club President Suspicious," *Spokesman-Review*, January 16, 1951.

33 Felix S. Cohen, "Erosion of Indian Rights, 1950–1953: A Case Study in Bureaucracy," *Yale Law Journal* 62 (Feb. 1953): 348–90. Felix Cohen, a champion of Indian rights and proficient legal scholar, made an important contribution to termination literature with this article, which Cohen wrote at the beginning of the federal government's termination efforts. He asked the government to understand that Indians are in a unique position within the United States and noted that the government should not use its advantage to impinge upon Indians' freedom. He also concluded that sovereignty meant that the original inherent powers held by Indian tribes had not been extinguished upon conquest (whether literal or political), and thus that tribes retained rights to inherent sovereignty issues such as self-government and community rules. Cohen's words reflect what many Colville tribal members said in an effort to retain their tribal recognition.

34 NARA DC, RG 75, Colville 054, CCF 2, box 21, folder 00-1953-054, part 1, Colville, "Agenda-Colville Business Council with Commissioner Glenn L. Emmons Yakima, Washington, submitted by James D. White, Chairman, Colville Business Council," October 10, 1953.

35 By January 1955 petitions advocating termination promised per capita payments ranging from $500 to $20,000 if the tribe liquidated. While the Colvilles obviously sought and found much useful information related to restoration and termination, misinformation also made its way into the mix. National Congress of American Indian records (hereafter NCAI), National Museum of the American Indian

Archives (hereafter NMAI), Smithsonian Institution (hereafter SI), box 103, "Petition to Support Termination, 1955" (n.d.).

36   NCAI, NMAI, SI, box 103, folder 3, "Summary of Views of Colville Delegates at Conference, Portland Area Office, April 1, 1955." A draft of the proposed restoration bill had apparently been circulated prior to this meeting, because the council minutes and the discussions reference it, but the bill was not included with the minutes. This draft bill included an interesting component—a payment of $40,000 annually to Ferry and Okanogan counties "for contribution by the Colville Indians to the counties . . . for services to the Indians." While this is interesting on its own merits, it becomes even more so in context of Public Law 280 (PL 280), which on August 15, 1953, transferred jurisdiction over Indian tribes in California, Minnesota (except the Red Lake Nation), Nebraska, Oregon (except the Warm Springs Reservation), Wisconsin (except later the Menominee Indian Reservation), and, upon its statehood, Alaska from the federal government to the state government. When PL 280 took effect in Washington in 1965, the Colville Tribes began to pay Ferry and Okanogan counties $40,000 a year to cover the costs of law enforcement.

37   Frederick Hoxie and Peter Iverson, eds., *Indians in American History: An Introduction* (Wheeling, IL: Harlan Davidson, 1998), 237.

38   Covington received assistance from the American Indian Press Association in creating *Our Heritage*, and through that relationship introduced the Colville termination debate to an even larger national group (*Indian Country Today*, March 28, 2003).

39   NARA DC, RG 75, Colville 054, box 21, folder 14300-1954-054 [2 of 2], "Letter from Henry M. Jackson U.S.S. to Honorable Glenn L. Emmons, December 7, 1954, with a response to Jackson on December 14, 1954, from W. Barton Greenwood, Acting Commissioner." Tribal members' reaching out to federal and elected officials as leaders of factions was problematic on other reservations during this period as well. In a 1955 letter to secretary of the Interior Douglas McKay, Elizabeth Roe Cloud, wife of Henry Roe Cloud, indicated that she knew that Wade Crawford, a member of the Klamath tribe and former superintendant of the Klamath reservation, had been in Washington, DC, and had said that he was acting on behalf of the Klamath Tribe. Roe Cloud reminded McKay that Crawford was not an elected representative of the Klamath Tribe, but instead led a pro-termination faction. Because Crawford had garnered much national attention, where he misrepresented the Klamath peoples' readiness for termination, Roe Cloud wondered if McKay might rein him in, but do so carefully, as he had found a national audience. NCAI, NMAI, SI, box 103, "Letter to the Honorable Douglas McKay from Elizabeth Roe Cloud, May 11, 1955."

40   NARA DC, RG 75, Colville 054, box 21, folder 14300-1954-054 [2 of 2], stamped "Received Interior Dept. Asst. Secy. December 7, 1954." Membership letter from Lucy Swan, secretary-treasurer of the CIA.

41   "3 Old Indian Chiefs Join in a Discussion of New Plan," *Spokane Daily Chronicle*, June 28, 1954.

42   NCAI, NMAI, SI, box 103, folder 9, "Meeting at Portland Area Office," April 1, 1955.

43   NCAI, NMAI, SI, box 103, folder 9, "Lawrence Nicodemus letter to David White," May 14, 1955. David White also used the name James D. White.

44 NCAI, NMAI, SI, box 103, folder 9, James D. "White letter to Lawrence Nicodemus," May 31, 1955.

45 NCAI, NMAI, SI, box 103, folder 9, "James D. White letter to Helen Peterson," June 9, 1955

46 The organization generally asserted its opposition to the policy in any form, despite calling Menominee termination a victory for that tribe in 1954 because the Menominees had "requested it." See David R. M. Beck *The Struggle for Self-Determination: History of the Menominee Indians since 1854*, 142n56.

47 Beginning in 1955 and for several years in a row, Colville Tribal Council resolutions authorizing payment of NCAI dues would pass by margins of only one vote. Finally, in 1963, when pro-terminationists won control of the Colville Business Council, the council stopped paying NCAI dues and withdrew the Colville Tribes from the organization. Individual Colville members maintained their personal memberships during this time, but the tribe would not formally reestablish the relationship until the mid-1970s.

48 Congress, House, Committee on Interior and Insular Affairs, Subcommittee on Indian Affairs, *Restoring to Tribal Ownership Certain Lands upon the Colville Indian Reservation, Washington, and for Other Purposes*, 84th Cong., 2nd sess., 1956.

49 "Report Due Tuesday," *Grand Coulee (WA) Star*, September 29, 1960.

50 In 1961 the Colville Tribes had approximately 4,500 members. Roughly 25 percent of the membership, 1125 people, lived on the reservation. Adults represent nearly half of the reservation population, which translates into 563 eligible voting members. Consequently, 65 percent of the local voting membership attended the two-day termination meeting. Modern meetings and elections often result in fewer than 20 percent participation, so the high attendance in 1961 takes on an even greater significance.

51 The Klamath and the Ute tribes also lacked the opportunity to vote yes or no on termination. Their processes both began with how to terminate, not whether they wanted to.

52 "Tribe Polled on Termination," *Spokesman-Review*, June 19, 1961.

53 National Archives Records Administration (NARA), Pacific Coast Branch (PCB), Record Group 75, box 1528, folders 1961, "Letter from Harvey Moses, Chairman, Colville Business Council, to the Honorable Stewart Udall, Secretary of the Interior," p. 1.

54 "Report on Status," *Spokane Daily Chronicle*, October 18, 1966.

55 NARA DC, RG 75, Colville 054, CCF 2, box 21, folder 00-1953-054, part 1, Colville, "Minutes, Special Session of the Business Council, May 27 and 28, 1954, Colville Indian Agency."

56 U.S. Census Current Population Consumer Income, series P-60, no. 15, April 27, 1954. See http://www2.census.gov/prod2/popscan/p60-015.pdf, retrieved April 12, 2011. NCAI, NMAI, SI, box 68, folder 10, "Statement of Paschal Sherman, Enrolled Member of the Colville Confederated Tribes in Opposition to H.R. 6154 and H.R. 7190, before the House of Representatives Subcommittee on Indian Affairs, July 22, 1955, 84th Congress, 1st Session."

57 The Grand Coulee Dam was built in 1933 on a Columbia River bed, half of which was owned by the tribe. In exchange for flooding traditional fishing areas like Kettle Falls, the federal government was supposed to pay for the land prior to breaking ground, and also promised free power and a percentage of all revenue generated by the sale of the electricity from the dam. Resolution of this agreement did not come until 1995, when Congress finally passed the 181 D claims bill. A lump sum payment was provided to each tribal member, and the tribe also receives a small percentage of annual profits from the electricity generated by the Grand Coulee Dam, but tribal members do not receive free electricity. This payment was sixty years overdue, and consequently two generations of Colvilles went without compensation for losing their land and fishing areas.

58 Paschal Sherman had grown up on the reservation but lived in Washington, DC, during the termination era. Sherman was the first tribal member to attain a PhD and he also held an LLB degree. He served as an officer of the National Congress of American Indians during the 1950s. Sherman had been born Frank Wapato, and his traditional name was Quas-quay or Bluejay, but a priest at the St. Mary's Mission school suggested he take the name Paschal Sherman. Paschal Sherman was the grandson of Chief John Wapato and was Wenatchi. Although he lived far removed from the reservation for most of his adult life, Sherman maintained close ties to the reservation and his fellow tribal members, and forged a relationship with many to create the Petitioners Party. T. B. Charley, of Malott—a reservation town between Okanogan and Brewster—led the Petitioners Party at the local level while Sherman fought against termination in Washington, DC. Upon Sherman's death in 1970, President Richard M. Nixon sent a telegram to his family, noting that Sherman's death "brings sorrow to the hearts of all who followed his inspiring life's career." Nixon offered his sympathy and asserted, "May the knowledge of his enduring achievements comfort you, even as it will continue to enrich our country and the people to whom he was devoted."

59 Congress, Senate, Committee on Interior and Insular Affairs, Subcommittee on Indian Affairs, S. 1442, S. 1169, 88th Cong., 1st sess., October 24, 25, and 26, 1963, 29.

60 According to W. Richard West Jr. and Kevin Gover, the policy of termination had been discredited by 1960. They indicated that President John F. Kennedy's meeting with Crow representatives in 1962 symbolized a turn away from termination. W. Richard West Jr. and Kevin Gover, "The Struggle for Indian Civil Rights," in Hoxie and Iverson, *Indians in American History*, 225–26.

61 Congress, Senate, Committee on Interior and Insular Affairs, Subcommittee on Indian Affairs, S. 1442, S. 1169, 88th Cong., 1st sess., October 24, 25, and 26, 1963, 22. It is not clear what data the commissioner reviewed related to education among Colville tribal members, because few had opportunities to engage in higher education at this time. He may have been referring mainly to off-reservation tribal members, some of whom would not have been raised on the reservation.

62 Covington is an excellent illustration of the complexities of the termination debate. As a member of the Moses band, one of the bands imposed upon the tribe, and a

mixed-blood, some tribal members might have questioned her Colville identity. Covington not only clearly identified as a Colville but also fought for years to preserve the reservation.

63 John Fahey, *Saving the Reservation: Joe Garry and the Battle to Be Indian* (Seattle: University of Washington Press, 2001), 195n18.

2. "IT IS LIKE GIVING YOUR EAGLE FEATHER AWAY."

1 National Archives Records Administration (NARA), Pacific Coast Branch (PC), Record Group (RG) 75, box 1528, folder 1961, "Meeting report," February 18–19, 1.

2 NARA, PC, RG 75, box 1528, folder 1961, "Meeting report," February 18–19, 8.

3 NARA, PC, RG 75, box 1528, folder 1961, comments from ballots, 1–4.

4 Ibid.

5 NARA, PC, RG 75, box 1528, folder 1961, ballot results.

6 NARA, PC, RG 75, box 1528, folder 1961, letter to secretary of Interior.

7 Demographically, of the 75 percent of the tribal members that resided off the reservation, with 25 percent living adjacent to or near the reservation, and 50 percent living removed from it. The adult population comprised roughly 40 percent of the total membership, and the majority of adults fell into the under-fifty-years-of-age category. NARA, PC, RG 75, box 1528, folder 1961, "Planning Report Number 3."

8 NARA, PC, box 1529, folder 1961, "Opinion Poll Number 1."

9 NARA, PC, box 1529, folder 1961, termination draft.

10 Congress, House, Committee on Interior and Insular Affairs, Subcommittee on Indian Affairs, H.R. 6801, H.R. 8469, 87th Cong., 2nd sess., May 15, 1962, 12.

11 Hearings, 15–17.

12 Ibid., 18.

13 Secretary of the Interior Stewart Udall appointed Nash to be his commissioner in August of 1961. Nash would hold the position until Robert Bennett assumed it in 1966. Nash had been on Udall's Task Force on Indian Affairs, a group charged with determining what kinds of initiatives and programs the Indians of America desired. Nash was an anthropologist by training and also had political experience as lieutenant governor of Wisconsin. He won the respect and trust of many tribal groups as he illustrated his interest in them and respect for them during his tenure. For more on Nash, see Francis Paul Prucha, *The Great Father* (Lincoln: University of Nebraska Press, 1995), 1090–91; and Margaret Connell Szasz, "Philleo Nash, 1961–66," in *The Commissioners of Indian Affairs, 1824–1977*, ed. Robert M. Kvasnicka and Herman J. Viola (Lincoln: University of Nebraska Press, 1979), 311–24.

14 For national context on this and similar issues, see Kenneth R. Philp, ed., *Indian Self-Rule: First-Hand Accounts of Indian-White Relations from Roosevelt to Reagan* (Logan: Utah State University Press, 1995).

15 Hearings, 21

16 Ibid., 23.

17 Ibid., 53.

18 NCAI, NMAI, SI, box 66, folder 6, press release, August 6, 1960.

19 NARA, PC, RG 75, box 1528, folder 1961, "Mrs. Marian Bourgeau of Inchelium letter to President Kennedy." Stewart Udall held the secretary of the Interior position from January 20, 1961, through January 23, 1969. Udall had served in the House of Representatives from Arizona and maintained a deep interest in Indian affairs. He supported Kennedy's mission to focus on economic development for Indians and on the move away from termination. For more on Udall see Prucha, *Great Father*, 1087–88.

20 Hearings, 11.

21 R. Warren Metcalf provided an excellent study of this anomalous situation in *Termination's Legacy: The Discarded Indians of Utah* (Lincoln: University of Nebraska Press, 2002).

22 Hearings, 27.

23 Ibid., 28.

24 The Coeur d'Alene tribal council and tribal members also remained concerned about Colville hunting and fishing rights throughout the debate, because the Colvilles and the Coeur d'Alene's enjoyed reciprocal access to hunting and fishing.

25 Hearings, 29.

26 Ibid., 33.

27 Ibid.

28 Arthur V. Watkins, "Termination of Federal Supervision: The Removal of Restrictions over Indian Property and Person," *Annals of the American Academy of Political and Social Science* 311 (May 1957): 48.

29 Watkins, "Termination of Federal Supervision," 50.

30 Colville Business Council Resolution 1955–35, Nespelem, WA.

31 Kathleen A. Dahl, "The Battle over Termination on the Colville Indian Reservation," *American Indian Culture and Research Journal*, no. 118 (1994): 29.

3. "SOON BURIED IN A JUNK PILE OF CADILLACS."

1 "Indians Weigh Termination," *Spokesman-Review*, April 3, 1963.

2 Congress, Senate, Committee on Interior and Insular Affairs, Subcommittee on Indian Affairs, S. 1442, S. 1169, 88th Cong., 1st sess., October 24, 25, 26, 1963, various letters throughout.

3 Ibid., 6.

4 Ibid., 20–21.

5 Ibid., 27.

6 Ibid., 30.

7 Ibid., 31.

8 Ibid., 34.

9 Ibid., 37.

10 Ibid.

11 Ibid., 39.

12 Ibid., 45.

13 Ibid., 52.

14 Ibid., 54–55.

15 Ibid., 57.

16 Ibid., 61.

17 Ibid., 71–74.

18 Ibid., 85–86.

19 Ibid., 98.

20 Ibid., 99.

21 Ibid., 100

22 Ibid., 113.

23 Ibid., 104.

24 Ibid., 105.

25 Ibid.

26 Ibid., 107.

27 Ibid., 113–15. The education numbers listed refer to a questionnaire sent to 2,167 adults on the tribal roll in the spring of 1961; 1,237 the surveys were returned.

28 Ibid., 147.

29 Ibid., 160.

30 Ibid., 196.

31 Ibid., 218.

32 Ibid., 221.

33 Ibid., 223.

34 Ibid., 244–45.

35 Ibid., 251.

36 Ibid., 266.

4. "WHAT IS THEIR FUTURE?"

1 Thomas S. Foley had been assistant attorney general for the state of Washington, then became assistant chief clerk and special counsel of the Committee on Interior and Insular Affairs of the Senate from 1961 to 1963. Foley served as the representative from Washington's Fifth Congressional District from 1965 to 1995, and became Speaker of the House of Representatives in 1993 (Biographical Directory of the United States Congress, http://bioguide.congress.gov, 2005). Foley maintained an interest in Indian affairs throughout his political career. For more on Foley, see Jeffrey R. Biggs and Thomas S. Foley, *Honor in the House: Speaker Tom Foley* (Pullman: Washington State University Press, 1999).

2 Congress, House, Committee on Interior and Insular Affairs, Subcommittee on Indian Affairs (hereafter referred to as Congress, House), H.R. 5925, S. 1413, H.R. 6331, 89th Cong., 1st sess., June 18; August 13; November 3, 4, 5, 1965, 1–10.

3 "Indian Group Attacks Horan for Viewpoints," *Omak Chronicle*, October 29, 1964.

4 "Council Elects CLP Chairman," *Omak Chronicle*, July 16, 1964.

5 "Tribe Splits Over Termination Bills," *Spokesman-Review*, November 6, 1965.

6 Congress, House, 11.

7 Ibid., 23. Odell served in Washington State District 4, located in Spokane County.

8   Ibid., 32.

9   Ibid., 33.

10   Ibid., 35.

11   Congress, Senate, Committee on Interior and Insular Affairs, Subcommittee on Indian Affairs, S. 282, 90th Cong., 1st sess., June 8, 1967, 119–20.

12   Congress, House, 75–76.

13   Ibid., 96.

14   Ibid., 112–13. Note: Tribal members whose land is held in trust by the tribe do not pay property taxes to the county. Tribal members who own land in fee status do pay taxes, just like any other landholder of fee title property.

15   Ibid., 120–22.

16   Ibid., 144–46.

17   Ibid., 151.

18   Ibid., 182, 176.

19   Ibid., 164.

20   Ibid., 172.

21   Ibid., 199.

22   Ibid., 201.

23   D'Arcy McNickle, one of the original members of the NCAI, founded in 1944, alerted Indians to the prevailing mood in Washington in 1947 and warned attendees at the NCAI's fourth annual convention that Indians must "stand together against the forces that would deprive them of their rights, their liberties, and their lands" (Peter Iverson, *We Are Still Here: American Indians in the Twentieth Century* [Wheeling, IL: Harlan Davidson, 1998]), 123. The NCAI's campaign raised non-Indian awareness of Indian issues and benefited all groups beyond the 1960s (Fredrick Hoxie and Peter Iverson, eds., *Indians in American History: An Introduction* [Wheeling, IL: Harlan Davidson, 1998], 207–8). For more on the NCAI, see N. B. Johnson, "The National Congress of American Indians," *American Indian* 3 (Summer 1946): 1–4; Johnson, "The National Congress of American Indians," *Chronicle of Oklahoma* 30 (Summer 1952): 140–48; Thomas W. Cowger, *The National Congress of American Indians: The Founding Years* (Lincoln: University of Nebraska Press, 1999).

24   John Fahey, *Saving the Reservation: Joe Garry and the Battle to Be Indian* (Seattle: University of Washington Press, 2001), 5.

25   Congress, House, 223.

26   Ibid., 223–24.

27   Ibid., 227.

28   Ibid., 235–36.

29   Ibid., 245–46.

30   Ibid., 286, 287.

31   "Indians Testify on Termination," *Wenatchee Daily World*, November 4, 1965.

32   Congress, House, 295–96.

33   Ibid.

34   George had been NCAI executive director from 1952 to 1953 and also cofounded the ATNI (Fahey, *Saving the Reservation*, 26–27).

35 Congress, House, 308.

36 Ibid., 314.

37 Ibid., 343.

38 Ibid., 346–48.

39 Ibid., 366–67.

40 "Area CIA Chapter Supports Council Bill," *Omak Chronicle*, September 3, 1964.

41 Congress, House, 379.

42 Ibid., 420.

43 Ibid., 422–24.

44 Ibid., 428.

45 Ibid., 434–35.

5. "COME BACK FROM YOUR PILGRIMAGE TO NOWHERE."

1 "The Colville Indian Reservation and the Pros and Cons of Termination," *Inland Catholic Register*, February 27, 1966.

2 Congress, Senate, Committee on Interior and Insular Affairs, Subcommittee on Indian Affairs (hereafter referred to as Congress, Senate), S. 282, 90th Cong., 1st sess., June 8, 1967, 20–21.

3 "Colville Indians Ponder Future at Meeting," *Wenatchee Daily World*, March 17, 1967.

4 "Commissioner Pledges Termination Support," *Omak Chronicle*, March 23, 1967.

5 NARA PC, RG 75, box 1530, folder 1967, "Minutes of March 17, 1967, Meeting," p. 2..

6 Ibid., 38.

7 Ibid., 40.

8 Congress, Senate, 2.

9 Ibid., 25–26.

10 "The Colville Indian Reservation and The Pros and Cons of Termination," *Inland Catholic Register*, February 20, 1966.

11 Congress, Senate, 192.

12 Ibid., 32.

13 Ibid., 35.

14 Dellwo became heavily involved with the protection of Indian rights to regulate non-Indian hunting and fishing on tribal lands, as well as the preservation of Indian cultural practices related to hunting and fishing. His advocacy during the 1960s and 1970s gained national attention and praise from Indian groups nationwide.

15 Ibid., 66.

16 Ibid., 70.

17 Ibid., 72.

18 Ibid., 76.

19 Ibid., 85

20 Ibid., 87–88. The official figure regarding the discrepancy between the initially agreed-upon termination amount and the actual per capita payment is roughly $15,000 per person.

21 Ibid., 91–92.

22 Ibid., 120.

23 Ibid., 125.

24 The National Indian Youth Council grew out of the American Indian Chicago
conference, held at the University of Chicago in 1961. This group of activists, led
by Clyde Warrior (Ponca) and several other Native American students, became
a major force in Indian activism throughout the 1960s and 1970s. Hank Adams
(Assiniboine) became a leading voice of the group during the fish-ins and battles
for Indian water rights in the Pacific Northwest. For more on Hank Adams, the
NIYC, and Native American activism, see Frederick Hoxie and Peter Iverson, *Indians
in American History: An Introduction* (Wheeling, IL: Harlan Davidson, Inc., 1998);
Kenneth R. Philp, ed., *Indian Self-Rule: First-Hand Accounts of Indian-White Relations
from Roosevelt to Reagan* (Logan: Utah State University Press, 1995); and Paul Chaat
Smith and Robert Allen Warrior, *Like a Hurricane: The Indian Movement from Alcatraz
to Wounded Knee* (New York: New Press, 1996); Daniel M. Cobb, *Native Activism in
Cold War America: the Struggle for Sovereignty* (Lawrence: University of Kansas Press,
2009).

25 Congress, Senate, 148.

26 Ibid., 148–49.

27 Ibid., 159.

28 "The Colville Indian Reservation and The Pros and Cons of Termination," *Inland
Catholic Register*, February 27, 1966.

29 Congress, Senate, 166.

30 "The Colville Indian Reservation and the Pros and Cons of Termination," *Inland
Catholic Register*, February 27, 1966.

31 Congress, Senate, 168.

32 Officials of the Reagan administration and president Ronald Reagan often characterized Indians and Indian reservations in this manner as well, two decades after
the termination era. Secretary of the Interior James Watt called reservations "a
failed experiment in socialism." Reagan, in a speech at Moscow State University on
May 31, 1988, indicated that perhaps the government had 'humored' the Indian too
long in his desire to remain true to Indian values. He suggested, "Maybe we should
have said no, come join us; be citizens along with the rest of us." *Indian Country
Today*, various issues, 1984–88.

33 Congress, Senate, 172.

34 Ibid., 186.

35 Ibid., 190.

36 Ibid., 173–74.

37 Ibid., 176.

38 Ibid., 184.

39 For more on similar representations of silence and language, see Keith Basso, *Wisdom Sits in Places: Landscape and Language among the Western Apache* (Albuquerque:
University of New Mexico, 1996).

6. "NOT ANOTHER INCH, NOT ANOTHER DROP."

1 Congress, House, Committee on Interior and Insular Affairs, Subcommittee on Indian Affairs (hereafter referred to as Congress, House), S. 282, 90th Cong., 2d sess., July 12, 1968, 71.

2 Ibid., 72.

3 Ibid., 79.

4 Ibid., 80.

5 Ibid., 91.

6 Haley asserted this repeatedly throughout the hearings in 1965, 1967, and 1968.

7 Congress, House, 105–6.

8 President Richard M. Nixon launched new Indian policies that included repudiating termination, allowing tribes to administer their own federal programs and their own educational initiatives, improving health care systems, and providing economic development opportunities for reservations alongside training programs for tribal members that would allow greater participation in tribal planning and corporations. These initiatives all fell under the auspices of self-determination, and breathed new life into tribal governments and programs.

9 Congress, House, 114–15.

10 Ibid., 122.

11 Ibid., 123.

12 Ibid., 144.

13 Ibid., 124.

14 Ibid., 127.

15 Executive Order 11399, "Establishing the National Council on Indian Opportunity," March 6, 1968, 33 *Federal Register* 4425 (March 7, 1967).

16 Congress, House, 128.

17 Ibid., 137.

18 Ibid., 138–39.

19 Ibid, 139–40.

20 Ibid., 143.

21 Ibid.

22 Ibid.

23 Ibid., 144.

24 Ibid., 146.

25 Ibid. Forbearance of property taxes had not been mentioned in prior hearings, so this was a new aspect of the termination settlement. Property taxation was one of the leading anxieties of termination opponents, because the Menominees had lost so much of their land base when they had to sell land in order to pay taxes.

26 Public Law 280 was passed in 1953 and can be seen as a companion to termination. Until P.L. 280, the federal government and tribal police enforced law and order on reservations. Passage of P.L. 280 transferred some of that jurisdiction to states. Initially, only six states were part of P.L. 280, but in the years following passage, ten states, including Washington, assumed some control over law and order on reservations.

27 Hearings, 149.

28 Ibid., 155.

29 Ibid., 156.

30 Ibid., 161, 164.

31 Ibid., 165–67.

32 Ibid., 173.

33 The tribe did win a judgment against the Bonneville Power Administration in 1995. The administration made a lump sum payment to the tribe, distributed as a per capita, and tribal members also receive a small annual per capita from the dam's revenues. These twin payments remain examples of the many claims, financial and cultural, that the tribes would have lost if termination had proceeded.

34 Congress, House, 173–74.

35 Vine Deloria Jr. and Clifford M. Lytle, eds., *American Indians, American Justice* (Austin: University of Texas Press, 1983), 20.

36 "Colville Indians Urged Not to Lose Reservation," *Wenatchee Daily World*, April 12, 1971. Stevens, a member of the Oneida Tribe of Wisconsin, recounted the Oneida experience with changing the reservation—they distributed land to individual tribal members and lost nearly the entire reservation. At that time, the tribe was fighting to get the land back. Another Oneida, Robert Bennett, had been advising the Colvilles to accelerate their termination plans as recently as 1967, and this shift indicates how far the bureau had turned away from the policy.

CONCLUSION. "WE KEPT GETTING A LITTLE BIT SMARTER

1   Jaakko Puisto, "This Is My Reservation, I Belong Here": The Salish Kootenai Struggle against Termination" (PhD diss., Arizona State University, 2000), 199.

2   Susan Hood, "Termination of the Klamath Tribe in Oregon," *Ethnohistory* 19 (Fall 1972): 380.

3   Ibid., 382.

4   Ibid., 388–89.

5   Hood, "Termination of the Klamath Tribe," 383.

6   Ibid., 386.

7   Ibid., 388.

8   Nicholas C. Peroff, *Menominee DRUMS: Tribal Termination and Restoration, 1954–1974* (Norman: University of Oklahoma Press, 1982), 52–54.

9   Ibid., 43–44, 54.

10 Ibid., 55.

11 Ibid., 56. This vote by 202 tribal members ended up representing the whole tribal membership, more than three thousand people.

12 Ibid., 58.

13 Ibid., 86.

14 Ibid., 89.

15 Ibid., 45–46.

16 Deer became assistant secretary of the Interior for Indian Affairs in 1993 (Hoxie

and Iverson, 283). For more on Ada Deer, see Peter Iverson, *"We Are Still Here":* *American Indians in the Twentieth Century* (Wheeling, IL: Harlan Davidson, 1998), 143, 201; and Kenneth Philp, *Indian Self-Rule: First-Hand Accounts of Indian-White Relations from Roosevelt to Reagan* (Logan: Utah State University Press, 1995), 231–34.

17 Peroff, *Menominee DRUMS,* 189–90.

18 Puisto, "This Is My Reservation," 210.

19 Ibid., 167, 180, 193, 197.

20 Ibid., 210–13.

21 Congress, House, Committee on Interior and Insular Affairs, Subcommittee on Indian Affairs, H.R. 5925, S. 1413, H.R. 6331, 89th Cong., 1st sess., June 18; August 13; November 3, 4, 5, 1965, 373.

22 R. Warren Metcalf, *Termination's Legacy: The Discarded Indians of Utah* (Lincoln: University of Nebraska Press, 2002), 87.

23 Ibid., 147.

24 Ibid., 180.

25 The Colvilles never seriously considered dividing the tribal membership by blood quantum. Some tribal members asserted that if the Colvilles did have to terminate because off-reservation (i.e., mixed-blood) tribal members wanted to, they hoped that reservation (i.e., full-blood) Colvilles would get a larger share of the sale revenue since they were "more" Indian. The mixed-bloods, of course, fought any distinction among blood degree, and the subcommittee never appeared to seriously consider it. Tribal members who did support division according to degree of Colville blood did not advocate cutting off access at any certain percentage but instead suggested that each person would get shares of the money according to their own blood quantum—one-eighth, one-half, full.

26 Metcalf, *Termination's Legacy,* 228.

27 David R. M. Beck, *Seeking Recognition: The Termination and Restoration of the Coos, Lower Umpqua, and Siuslaw Indians, 1855–1984* (Lincoln: University of Nebraska Press, 2009), 96–106.

28 Ibid., 113–14.

29 Ibid., 161, 167.

30 Ibid., 195–202

31 Ibid., 207.

REFERENCES

MANUSCRIPTS, ARCHIVAL COLLECTIONS,
AND GOVERNMENT DOCUMENTS

Exec. Order No. 11399, "Establishing the National Council on Indian Opportunity," March 6, 1968, 33 Fed. Reg. 4425 (March 7, 1967).

Harmon, Alexandra. N.p., n.d. Author's collection.

H.R. Rep. Nos. 6801 and 8469. House Subcommittee on Indian Affairs of the House Committee on Interior and Insular Affairs. 87th Cong., 2nd sess. (May 15, 1962).

H.R. Rep. No. 5925; S. Doc. No. 1413; H.R. Rep. No. 6331. House Subcommittee on Indian Affairs of the House Committee on Interior and Insular Affairs. 89th Cong., 1st sess. (June 18; August 13; November 3, 4, 5, 1965).

H.R. Rep. No. 3051 and S. Doc. No. 282. Hearing before the Subcommittee on Indian Affairs of the Committee on Interior and Insular Affairs House of Representatives. 90th Cong., 2nd sess. (July 12, 1968).

McAdams Webster, John, Papers. Cage 145, Washington State University, Holland and Terrell Libraries, Manuscripts, Archives, and Special Collections (MASC), Pullman, WA.

National Archives Records Administration, Seattle, WA. Record Group 75. Colville Confederated Tribe, box 1528, folders 1961, 1962; box 1530.

National Archives Records Administration, Washington, DC. Record Group 75. Colville Confederated Tribe, Central Classified File, Colville 054, boxes 20–22.

National Congress of American Indian. Records. National Museum of the American Indian Archives, Smithsonian Institution, Suitland, MD.

S. Doc. No. 282. Hearing before the Subcommittee on Indian Affairs of the Committee on Interior and Insular Affairs United States Senate. 90th Cong., 1st sess. (June 8, 1967).

U.S. Congress, House. *Restoring to Tribal Ownership Certain Lands upon the Colville Indian Reservation, Washington, and for Other Purposes*. House Subcommittee on Indian Affairs of the House Committee on Interior and Insular Affairs. 84th Cong., 2nd sess. (1956).

U.S. Congress, Senate. S. Doc. Nos. 1442 and 1169. Hearings before the Subcommittee on Indian Affairs of the Committee on Interior and Insular Affairs United States Senate. 88th Cong., 1st sess. (October 24, 25, and 26, 1963).

Wapato, Paul. "Paschal Sherman Memorial." May 29, 1998. Author's collection.

Watt, Darlena. 125th Anniversary of Colville Confederated Tribes. Commemoration Speech, July 11, 1997.

Winans, W. P., Papers. Cage 147, Washington State University Holland and Terrell Library. Manuscripts, Archives, and Special Collections, Pullman, WA.

ARTICLES, BOOKS, AND DISSERTATIONS

Ames, David W., and Burton R. Fisher. "The Menominee Termination Crisis: Barriers in the Way of a Rapid Cultural Transition." *Human Organization* 18 (Fall 1959): 101–11.

Badger, Anthony J. *The New Deal: The Depression Years, 1933–1940.* Lanham, MD: Ivan R. Dee, 2002.

Basso, Keith. *Wisdom Sits in Places: Landscape and Language among the Western Apache.* Albuquerque: University of New Mexico, 1996.

Beck, David R. M. *Seeking Recognition: The Termination and Restoration of the Coos, Lower Umpqua, and Siuslaw Indians, 1855–1984.* Lincoln: University of Nebraska Press, 2009.

———. *The Struggle for Self-Determination: History of the Menominee Indians since 1854.* Lincoln: University of Nebraska Press, 2005.

Biggs, Jeffrey R., and Thomas S. Foley. *Honor in the House: Speaker Tom Foley.* Pullman: Washington State University Press, 1999.

Boender, Debra R. "Termination and the Administration of Glenn L. Emmons as Commissioner of Indian Affairs, 1953–1961." *New Mexico Historical Review* 54 (Oct. 1979): 287–304.

Brophy, William A., and Sophie D. Aberle. *The Indian: America's Unfinished Business.* Norman: University of Oklahoma Press, 1966.

Burt, Larry. *Tribalism in Crisis: Federal Indian Policy, 1953–1961.* Albuquerque: University of New Mexico Press, 1982.

Carter, Kent. *The Dawes Commission and the Allotment of the Five Civilized Tribes, 1893–1914.* Orem, UT: Ancestry Publishing, 1999.

Cattelino, Jessica R. *High Stakes: Florida Seminole Gaming and Sovereignty.* Durham, NC: Duke University Press, 2008.

Clark, Blue. *Indian Tribes of Oklahoma: A Guide.* Civilization of the American Indian series. Norman: University of Oklahoma Press, 2009.

Cobb, Daniel M. *Native Activism in Cold War America: The Struggle for Sovereignty.* Lawrence: University Press of Kansas, 2009.

Cohen, Felix S. "Americanizing the White Man." *American Scholar* 21 (Spring 1952): 177–91.

———. "Erosion of Indian Rights, 1950–1953: A Case Study in Bureaucracy." *Yale Law Journal* 62 (Feb. 1953): 348–90.

———. "Indian Wardship: The Twilight of a Myth." *American Indian* 6 (Summer 1953): 8–14.

Connell Szasz, Margaret. "Philleo Nash, 1961–66." In *The Commissioners of Indian Affairs*, edited by Robert Kvasnicka and Herman Viola. Lincoln: University of Nebraska Press, 1979.

Cornell, Stephen. *The Return of the Native: American Indian Political Resurgence.* New York: Oxford University Press, 1988.

Cowger, Thomas W. *The National Congress of American Indians: The Founding Years*. Lincoln: University of Nebraska Press, 1999.

Dahl, Kathleen A. "The Battle over Termination on the Colville Indian Reservation." *American Indian Culture and Research Journal*, no. 118 (1994): 29–44.

Deloria, Phillip J. *Playing Indian*. New Haven: Yale University Press, 1998.

Deloria, Vine, Jr. *American Indian Policy in the Twentieth Century*. Norman: University of Oklahoma Press, 1985.

———. *Behind the Trail of Broken Treaties: An Indian Declaration of Independence*. Austin: University of Texas Press, 1985.

———. "Comfortable Fictions and the Struggle for Turf: An Essay Review of *The Invented Indian: Cultural Fictions and Government Policies*." In *Natives and Academics: Researching and Writing about American Indians*, edited by Devon A. Mihesuah, 65–83. Lincoln: University of Nebraska Press, 1998.

———. *Custer Died for Your Sins*. New York: Macmillan, 1969.

———. *The Nations Within: The Past and Future of American Indian Sovereignty*. Austin: University of Texas Press, 1984.

Deloria, Vine, Jr., and Clifford M. Lytle, eds. *American Indians, American Justice*. Austin: University of Texas Press, 1983.

Dippie, Brian W. *The Vanishing American: White Attitudes and U.S. Indian Policy*. Lawrence: University Press of Kansas, 1991.

du Lac, Thomas. "The Work of the Indian Claims Commission under the Act of 1946." *Pacific Historical Quarterly* 7 (April 1976): 125–42.

Fahey, John. *Saving the Reservation: Joe Garry and the Battle to Be Indian*. Seattle: University of Washington Press, 2001.

Fisher, Andrew H. *Shadow Tribe: The Making of Columbia River Identity*. Seattle: University of Washington Press, 2010.

Fixico, Donald. *Termination and Relocation: Federal Indian Policy, 1945–1960*. Albuquerque: University of New Mexico Press, 1986.

Fowler, Loretta. *Tribal Sovereignty and the Historical Imagination: Cheyenne-Arapaho Politics*. Lincoln: University of Nebraska Press, 2002.

Gidley, M. *With One Sky above Us: Life on an American Indian Reservation at the Turn of the Century*. New York: Putnam, 1979.

Gwydir, Rickard H. *Recollections from the Colville Indian Agency, 1886–1889*. Spokane, WA: Arthur H. Clark Company, 2001.

Hagan, William T. "Full Blood, Mixed Blood, Generic, and Ersatz: The Problem of Indian Identity." *Arizona and the West* 27 (Winter 1985): 309–26.

Harmon, Alexandra. *Indians in the Making: Ethnic Relations and Indian Identities around Puget Sound*. Berkeley: University of California Press, 1998.

Hasse, Larry. "Termination and Assimilation: Federal Indian Policy, 1943 to 1961." PhD diss., Washington State University, 1974.

Hood, Susan. "Termination of the Klamath Tribe in Oregon." *Ethnohistory* 19 (Fall 1972): 379–92.

Hoxie, Frederick. *A Final Promise: The Campaign to Assimilate the Indians, 1880–1920*. Lincoln: Bison Books for University of Nebraska Press, 2001.

Hoxie, Frederick, and Peter Iverson, eds. *Indians in American History: An Introduction.* Wheeling, IL: Harlan Davidson, 1998.

Iverson, Peter. *Diné:A History of the Navajos.* Albuquerque: University of New Mexico Press, 2002.

———, ed. *"For Our Navajo People": Diné Letters, Speeches, and Petitions, 1900–1960.* Albuquerque: University of New Mexico Press, 2002.

———. *"We Are Still Here": American Indians in the Twentieth Century.* Wheeling, IL: Harlan Davidson, 1998.

Johnson, N. B. "The National Congress of American Indians." *American Indian* 3 (Summer 1946): 1–4.

———. "The National Congress of American Indians." *Chronicle of Oklahoma* 30 (Summer 1952): 140–48.

Kickingbird, Kirke, and Karen Ducheneaux. *One Hundred Million Acres.* New York: Macmillan Publishing Co., 1973.

Koppes, Clayton R. "From New Deal to Termination: Liberalism and Indian Policy, 1933–1953." *Pacific Historical Review* 46 (Nov. 1977): 543–66.

Kvasnicka, Robert M., and Herman J. Viola, eds. *The Commissioners of Indian Affairs, 1824–1977.* Lincoln: University of Nebraska Press, 1979.

La Farge, Oliver. "Termination of Federal Supervision: Disintegration and the American Indians." *Annals of the American Academy of Political and Social Science* 311 (May 1957): 41–44.

Leuchtenburg, William E. *Franklin D. Roosevelt and The New Deal.* New York: Harper Perennial, 1963.

Lurie, Nancy O. "The Indian Claims Commission Act." *Annals of the American Academy of Political and Social Science* 311 (May 1957): 56–70.

———. "Menominee Termination: From Reservation to Colony." *Human Organization* 31 (Fall 1972): 257–70.

McNickle, D'Arcy. *American Tribalism: Indian Survivals and Indian Renewals.* New York: Oxford University Press, 1973.

———. *Indian Tribes of the United States: Ethnic and Cultural Survival.* London: Oxford University Press, 1968.

Metcalf, R. Warren. *Termination's Legacy: The Discarded Indians of Utah.* Lincoln: University of Nebraska Press, 2002.

Meyer, Melissa L. "American Indian Blood Quantum Requirements: Blood Is Thicker than Family." In *Over the Edge: Remapping the American West,* edited by Valerie Matsumoto and Blake Allmendinger, 231–44. Berkeley: University of California Press, 1999.

Mihesuah, Devon A., ed. *Natives and Academics: Researching and Writing about American Indians.* Lincoln: University of Nebraska Press, 1998.

Morrill, Angela. "Decolonizing Klamath Termination: Factionalism in Klamath Termination Discourse." Master's thesis, University of California, San Diego, 2008.

Myer, Dillon S. "Indian Administration: Problems and Goals." *Social Service Review* 27 (June 1953): 193–200.

Nagle, Joane. *American Indian Ethnic Renewal: Red Power and the Resurgences of Identity and Culture*. New York: Oxford University Press, 1998.

Officer, James E. "The Bureau of Indian Affairs since 1945: An Assessment." *Annals of the American Academy of Political and Social Science,* special issue, *American Indians Today* 436 (Mar. 1978): 61–72.

Orfield, Gary. *A Study of Termination Policy.* Chicago: University of Chicago Press, 1966.

Peroff, Nicholas C. *Menominee DRUMS: Tribal Termination and Restoration, 1954–1974.* Norman: University of Oklahoma Press, 1982.

Philp, Kenneth R. "Dillon S. Myer and the Advent of Termination: 1950–1953." *Western Historical Quarterly* 19, no. 1 (Jan. 1988): 37–59.

———, ed. *Indian Self-Rule: First-Hand Accounts of Indian-White Relations from Roosevelt to Reagan.* Logan: Utah State University Press, 1995.

———. *John Collier's Crusade for Indian Reform.* Tucson: University of Arizona Press, 1977.

———. *Termination Revisited: American Indians on the Trail to Self-Determination, 1933–1953.* Lincoln: University of Nebraska Press, 1999.

Pommersheim, Frank. *Broken Landscapes: Indians, Indian Tribes, and the Constitution.* New York: Oxford University Press, 2009.

Prucha, Francis Paul. *The Great Father: The United States Government and the American Indians*, vols. 1 and 2, unabridged. Lincoln: University of Nebraska Press, 1995.

Puisto, Jaakko. "'This Is My Reservation, I Belong Here': The Salish Kootenai Struggle Against Termination." PhD diss., Arizona State University, 2000.

Reichwein, Jeffrey C. *Emergence of Native American Nationalism in the Columbia Plateau.* New York: Garland Publishing, 1990.

Rich Lewis, David. "Still Native: The Significance of Native Americans in the History of the Twentieth-Century American West." *Western Historical Quarterly* 24, no. 2 (May 1993): 203–27.

Rosenthal, Harvey D. *Their Day in Court: A History of the Indian Claims Commission.* New York: Garland Publishing, 1990.

Rosier, Paul C. *Rebirth of the Blackfeet Nation, 1912–1954.* Lincoln: University of Nebraska Press, 2001.

———. "'They Are Ancestral Homelands': Race, Place, and Politics in Cold War Native America, 1945–1961." *Journal of American History* 92, no. 4 (March 2006): 1300–26.

Ross, John Alan. "Factionalism on the Colville Reservation." PhD diss., Washington State University, 1967.

Ruby, Robert H., and John A. Brown. *Half-Sun on the Columbia: A Biography of Chief Moses.* Norman: University of Oklahoma Press, 1965.

Rusco, Elmer. *A Fateful Time: The Background and Legislative History of the Indian Reorganization Act.* Reno: University of Nevada Press, 2000.

Smith, Paul Chaat, and Robert Allen Warrior. *Like a Hurricane: The Indian Movement from Alcatraz to Wounded Knee.* New York: New Press, 1996.

Sutton, Imre, ed. *Irredeemable America: The Indians' Estate and Land Claims.* Albuquerque: University of New Mexico Press, 1985.

Tyler, S. Lyman. "William A. Brophy, 1945–48." In *The Commissioners of Indian Affairs, 1824–1977,* edited by Robert M. Kvasnicka and Herman J. Viola. Lincoln: University of Nebraska Press, 1979.

Ulrich, Roberta. *American Indian Nations from Termination to Restoration, 1953–2006.* Lincoln: University of Nebraska Press, 2010.

Walch, Michael C. "Terminating the Indian Termination Policy." *Stanford Law Review* 35, no. 6 (Jul. 1983): 1181–215.

Watkins, Arthur V. "Termination of Federal Supervision: The Removal of Restrictions over Indian Property and Person." *Annals of the American Academy of Political and Social Science* 311 (May 1957): 47–55.

Wilkinson, Charles F. *American Indians, Time, and the Law.* New Haven, CN: Yale University Press, 1988.

———. *Blood Struggle: The Rise of Modern Indian Nations.* New York: W. W. Norton and Company, 2005.

Wilkinson, Charles F., and Eric R. Biggs. "The Evolution of the Termination Policy." *American Indian Law Review* 5 (1977): 139–84.

Zimmerman, William, Jr. "The Role of the Bureau of Indian Affairs since 1933." *Annals of the American Academy of Political and Social Science* 311 (May 1957): 31–40.

INDEX

Pages with illustrations are shown in boldface type.

BIA and, 27; campaign letter for, **70**; campaigns by, 27–28; domination by, 95; platform of, **71**; poster for, **69**; and termination, 28, 116

Colville Reservation, xiii, 11, 29, 34, 65, 73, 113, 116, 123, 127, 147; debate on, xiv-xv; establishment and growth of, 4–7; hearings on, 49; map of, **viii**; property interests on, 117; social services on, 104; South End of, **ii**; and termination, 16, 17, 27; unrest on, 3–4

Colville Statesman-Examiner, 83

Colville Tribal Constitution, 12, 86

Colville Tribal Council, 22, 46, 101, 135, 154n47; campaign by, 40–41

Colville Tribal Enterprises Corporation (CTEC), 144

Committee on Indian Rights, 121–22

Confederated Salish and Kootenai Tribes, xi, 7, 15, 43, 135–36, 148n2; special rights for, 136; and termination, 137

Cook, Dibbon, 62

Coos, Lower Umpqua, and Siuslaw Restoration Act (1984), 142

Coos Tribe, xi, 136; recognition of, 141; and termination, 15, 142

Costain, Suzette, 64

Coulee Corridor, **32**

Council of Economic Advisers, 56

Court of Claims, US, 141, 151n21

Court of Indian Affairs, 11

Covington, Louis, 65

Covington, Lucy, xvi, 30, 84, 124, 153n38, 155n62; allocation of assets and, 114–15; and *Our Heritage,* 20; and termination, 29–30, 47–48, 85, 88, 114, 116

Crawford, Wade, 130, 153n39

Crossland, Mrs. Leo, 35

culture, 11, 42, 98, 107, 117, 118, 128, 160n4; assimilation and, 9; non-Indian, 100; tolerance for, 87

Curlew, Billy, 18

Curry, Rex, 140

D

Dawes, Henry L., 149n3, 149n13

Dawes Act (1887), 9, 10, 149n13

DeCamp, Virginia, 66

Deer, Ada, 135, 163n16

Dellwo, Robert, 99, 100, 160n14

Deloria, Vine, Jr., 29, 104

Democratic National Committee, 42

Department of Agriculture, 39, 40, 113, 130

Department of Justice, 9, 67

Department of the Budget, 40, 130

Department of the Interior, 13, 38, 39, 40, 41, 43, 45, 48, 56, 81, 97; and hunting/fishing rights, 57; and termination, 14, 15, 75, 95

Department of Veterans Affairs, 52

distribution, 28, 33, 54, 57, 114–15; vote for, 24

DRUMS. *See* Menominee DRUMS

E

economic development, 19, 25, 34, 39, 61, 75–76, 101–2, 114, 139; funding for, 124; regional, 120–21

Economic Development Administration, 121

education, 10, 11, 34, 47, 48, 75, 79, 88, 103, 105, 114, 134; funding for, 124; and termination, 122

Eisenhower, Dwight D., 104, 133

Emmons, Glenn, 13, 14, 16, 17

Empire Treaty (1855), 141

employment, 88, 104, 134; and termination, 78; timber-related, 134

Entiat band, 5, 80, 149n8

F

factionalism, 15–16

Federal Register, 57

Ferry County, 14, 22, 46, 102, 119, 121, 136

I

ICC. *See* Indian Claims Commission

Ickes, Harold, 12, 151n21

identity, 36, 65, 119, 132; decrease in, 9; group, xiv, 105; individual, 7; questions of, 17, 105; tribal, 99

Inchelium, 12, 53, 94, 150n19

Indian Bureau, 37, 41, 49, 53, 58, 83, 102, 113, 120

Indian Claims Commission (ICC), 47, 122, 141, 151n21; establishment of, 12; Klamaths and, 39; and termination, 18–19

Indian Health Service, xiii

Indian Reorganization Act (IRA), ix, 3, 10, 47, 77, 141, 150n15; Colville Indians and, 11–12; opposition to, 99; and termination, 28

Inks, Norma, 59, 79, 101–2

integration, 11, 99, 103

Inter-Tribal Council of Arizona, 22

IRA. *See* Indian Reorganization Act

Irwin, Robert, 87, 88, 103, 120

J

Jackson, Andrew, 10

Jackson, Charles, 80

Jackson, Henry M., 85, 151n26; CIA and, 20; H.C.R. 108 and, 147n1

James, Jim, 18, 21, 107

job training, 34, 47, 48

Johnson, Lyndon B., 103, 116

Johnson, Martha, 59, 84

Joseph, Chief, 5, 6, 90, 148n5

Joseph the Elder, 6

K

Kalispel Indians, 99; and termination, 100

Kamiakin, Cleveland, 21, 84

Keller, Washington, xii-xiii, 4–5, 51, 92, 150n19

Keller district, 12, 53

Kennedy, John F., 43, 52, 60, 64, 67; Crow representatives and, 155n60; Indian affairs and, 42, 103; mission of, 157n19

Kennedy, Robert F., 42, 67

Kettle Falls, 4, 36, 148n3, 155n57

Klamath Indians, 29, 53, 153n39; cultural quandary for, 128; designation for, 127; general assessment of, 128; and termination, ix, x, 16, 19–21, 24, 26, 33, 39, 40, 46–48, 55, 62, 63, 68, 73–74, 79, 97, 100, 102, 108, 117, 119, 120, 127–33, 138, 143; timber and, 102, 128, 129; tribal recognition and, 140

Klamath Reservation, 127, 132

Klamath Restoration Act (1986), 131

Kootenai Tribe. *See* Confederated Salish and Kootenai Tribes

L

Laird, Melvin, 132, 133

Lakes band, 7, 21, 36, 58, 64, 82, 105

land sales, 64, 79, 86

Landreth, Betty, and termination, 81

Lawrence, Alice, 113–14

Lemery, Mary, 121–22

liquidation, 25, 33, 36, 44, 52, 94, 114, 118, 152n35; assessing, 35; concerns about, 86–87; opposition to, 28, 61, 65, 84; single-option, 48–49; support for, 37, 98; timber, 38

Lone Wolf v. Hitchcock, 149n14, 150n14

Louie, Mary Catherine, 83

Lower Umpqua, xi, 136; recognition of, 141; and termination, 15, 142

Lum, Ira H., 27, 70

M

Malone, George, 20

McKay, Douglas, 153n39

McKinley, Francis, 139–40

McLaughlin, James, 9–10, 149n14

McLaughlin Agreement, 148n5

McNickle, D'Arcy, 159n23

membership, tribal: blood quantum and, 117; off-reservation, 51, 81, 105, 44, 164n25; questions of, 98; reservation, xi, 114, 134, 163n11

Menominee Advisory Council, 131

Menominee DRUMS (Determination of Rights and Unity for Menominee Shareholders), xi, 135

Menominee Enterprises, Incorporated (MEI), 135

Menominee General Council, 131

Menominee Indian Reservation, 132, 153n36

Menominee Restoration Act (1973), 135

Menominees, 162n25; county assistance for, 76; divisions among, 152n30; financial foundation of, 134; land/ tribal enterprises and, 29; recognition and, 140; restoration and, x; suit by, 131; and termination, ix, 19, 26, 40, 46–48, 55, 68, 102, 108, 117, 119, 120, 127, 131–35, 138, 143, 154n46

Menominee Termination Act (1954), 135

Metcalf, R. Warren, 140, 157n21

Methow band, 5, 149n8

mineral rights, 34, 35, 54, 64, 102, 122

mixed-bloods, xi, 86, 136, 139, 150n16, 164n25; and termination, 16, 138, 140; tribal government and, 25

Modoc band, 127

Moore, Frank, 40–41

Moore, L. Q., 62

Moses, Chief, 29, 83, 84, 85, 90, 95, 148n6; and Chief Joseph, 5; kinship ties and, 6

Moses, Harvey, 35, 59, 74, 94; on H.R. 4918, 61; on legal/moral obligations, 101; on S. 1442, 54; and termination, 85, 101

Moses, Madeline, 83, 95

Moses, Peter Dan, 18

Moses band, 5, 155n62

Moses-Columbia band, 18, 80, 148n6, 150n16

Muench, John, Jr., 121

Murray, James, 137

Myer, Dillon S., 13, 150n16

N

Nash, Philleo, 29, 40, 44, 45, 46, 156n13

National Congress of American Indians (NCAI), 29, 30, 41, 86, 104, 139, 152n35, 154n47, 155n58, 159n23, 159n34; Colville withdrawal from, xv, 22–23, 82; resolution by, 117; Sherman and, 52; and termination, xv, 23, 42, 117

National Forest Products Association, 121

National Indian Youth Council (NIYC), 103–4, 161n24

National Museum of the American Indian Archives (NMAI), xvi, xviii, 152–53n35

NCAI. *See* National Congress of American Indians

Nelson, Ronald, 58, 101, 120, 121

Nespelem, 12, 17, 35, 51, 53, 59, 88, 94; hearings in, 60, 63, 64, 81, 84–85, 95; landscape east of, **2**

Nespelem band, 5, 7, 147n4

Nespelem Indian Commercial Club, 16

Nez Perce Indians, 5, 80, 81, 90, 150n16; language of, 7; non-treaty, 6

Nez Perce Reservation, 5–6

Nez Perce Tribal Council, 80

Nicholas, Victor, 21

Nicholson, Barbara White, 77; and termination, 102–3, 117

Nicholson, Mary, 65

Nicholson, Narcisse, Jr., 69, 71, 74, 116; communal ownership and, 112; and termination, 78, 81–82, 112–13; testimony of, 98–99

Nicodemus, Lawrence, 22, 23

Nixon, Richard M., 124, 155n58, 162n8

water rights, 34, 45, 55

Watkins, Arthur, 46, 132; and termina-
    tion, 47, 133, 134–35, 137–40

Watt, Darlena "Doll," 150–51n20

Watt, James, 161n32

Webster, John McAdams, v, 147; on
    government interference, 9; San Poil
    band and, 18

welfare, x, 46, 59, 63, 64, 76, 81, 136

Wells Dam, dispute over, 124

Wenatchi band, 6, 149n8, 155n58

West, W. Richard, Jr., 155n60

Western Intertribal Coordinating Coun-
    cil, 82

Wheeler, Burton K., 150n15

Wheeler-Howard Act (IRA), 141, 150n15

White, James D., 18, 22

Whiteriver Tribe, 44, 139; and termina-
    tion, 138

Wicks, Joseph, 137

Williams, Charley, 107

Wilson, Sadie Moses, 90, 95

withdrawal, 18, 48, 79, 94, 99; plan for,
    14, 139

Y

Yahooskin band. *See* Snake Indians

Yakama Reservation, xv, 13, 27, 79, 80

Yakama Treaty, 148n1

Yakama Tribe, 80, 81; recognition and, 27

Z

Zimmerman, William, 131

CPSIA information can be obtained
at www.ICGtesting.com
Printed in the USA
FSHW022020101119
63959FS

9 780295 992280